Magnificen

They Wrote About
Cape Breton

Magnificent Obsessions

They Wrote About Cape Breton

EDITED WITH AN INTRODUCTION BY

Ronald Caplan

Breton Books

Editor: Ronald Caplan
Production Assistant: Bonnie Thompson
Layout: Fader Communications

 **Canada Council Conseil des Arts
for the Arts du Canada**
We acknowledge the support of the
Canada Council for the Arts for our publishing program.

We also acknowledge support from Cultural Affairs,
Nova Scotia Department of Tourism, Culture and Heritage.

Tourism, Culture and Heritage

We acknowledge the financial support of the
Government of Canada through the Canada Book
Fund for our publishing activities.

Library and Archives Canada Cataloguing in Publication

Magnificent obsessions : they wrote about Cape Breton / Ronald Caplan,
editor.

ISBN 978-1-895415-96-4

1. Cape Breton Island (N.S.)--History. 2. Cape Breton Island
(N.S.)--Civilization. 3. Micmac Indians--Nova Scotia--Cape Breton Island. I.
Caplan, Ronald, 1942-

FC2343.M34 2010   971.6'9   C2010-906281-7

Printed in Canada

CONTENTS

Introduction by Ronald Caplan

Introduction

IT IS A PLEASURE TO OFFER this collection that I have long carried as one carries song or poetry — batches of ideas I can call up and mull during a walk, or in conversation, or even in my dreams. These essays are offered as rich, lasting reading — perhaps even a sort of bedside book — each contributing to the portrait of Cape Breton Island.

A lot of my life, especially during the years of *Cape Breton's Magazine*, depended on the generous help of people who devoted themselves deeply to the island — people who became utterly consumed, and who, eventually, came back to us with the treasures they found, evidence of journeys they dared. I cannot be anything but grateful.

These people have devoted a good piece of their lives — and then we give each of them 15 or 20 delightful minutes, time that just might last the rest of our lives.

This book, *Magnificent Obsessions*, is offered in thanks to those who gave their lives to their obsessions, usually for little more reward than the pursuit itself.

I often think of Mary Willa Littler and her search for evidence to further her conclusions as to who is buried in The Strangers' Grave. Why does the demon not let her go? Or again, long ago Billy Joe Mac-Lean, Mayor of Port Hawkesbury, sent me across the Strait of Canso to get Leonard O'Neil, former Mayor of Mulgrave, to tell a forgotten story so vital to Cape Breton's economic future. Leonard had seen his efforts come to fruition, and I got to witness the achievement, the peace in his eyes.

Flora McPherson's chapter started with a phone call, a casual remark. I was about to publish a new edition of her classic book about Rev. Norman McLeod, *Watchman Against the World*. It occurred to me to ask, "What made you take on this particular subject? You had never been to Cape Breton, your people were not followers of Norman — and yet you took up the trail of a man both revered and despised." Her reply is in these pages.

Charles Burke is an historian who tells the story of Irish convicts dumped on Cape Breton's winter shore. Charles was himself captured when young, when a relative told him just enough of the story that it would never let him go. And yet again, there's David Dow from England, brought in as an idea man for DEVCO (the Cape Breton Development Corporation). They wanted him to find what is interesting about the island—information to inspire local people, to help lure tourists and fill out their visit. And away went David, asking and seeking, reading and talking—eventually sharing what he found in quirky little conversations on CBC morning radio—little talks worth waking up for.

Calvin Martin's achievement in these pages is a piece of writing that will not let me go—the poignancy of what happened when the Mi'kmaw kitchen became portable, when food no longer depended on boiling in a hollowed fallen tree but could be cooked in an easily transportable copper pot that was made in France. That trade good was certainly not the only thing that revolutionized and imperiled Mi'kmaw traditional life, but it is an achingly simple change that had severe economic, tribal, and spiritual consequences. It is a heartbreaking chapter.

I won't try to explain why I chose every chapter. They each speak eloquently for themselves. But I am certainly grateful to have found each of them, and to have this opportunity to share.

Ronald Caplan
Wreck Cove

The Meteorite That Shaped Cape Breton

David Dow

C APE BRETON ISLAND IS SO BEAUTIFUL that it is rare for anyone to ask why it is like it is. But if you do ask the question, you will find that there is much more to Cape Breton than meets the eye. For example, the Bras d'Or Lakes are salt, and you might think that this is quite normal since they are connected to the open sea. But when you start calculating the amount of rainfall, the amount of fresh water entering the Lakes, and the amount of sea water entering the Lakes, you find that the amount of salt required is about 24 million tons per year short, and the Lakes should be fresh water—not salt.

Magnificent Obsessions

So you search around and you find that at various places there are streams of brine welling up under the lake, and it is these that keep it salt. Perhaps you get to wondering how long you can go on extracting 24 million tons of salt per year from whatever deposit lies under the Lakes, and what would happen if the supply of salt did run out.

Then maybe you start to wonder not only why the Lakes are salt, but why the lake is there at all. You may, like myself, put two and two together and come up with the answer of four—sometimes twenty-two depending on your mood—and think that your answer is right and may be interesting to other people and so you decide to write it all down, not with the idea, of course, of stating flatly that "*This* is the way it happened," but rather, "This is the way it *might* have happened."

In the remote ages of the Earth, according to recent theories, all the great continents were joined together in one huge land mass, which finally broke up into the continents which are known today.

The continent of the Americas drifted slowly away from what is now Europe and Africa, leaving a great gulf which filled with water and became the Atlantic Ocean. Cape Breton apparently trailed along behind the main mass rather like a chip of wood which rides along behind a floating log. If you look carefully at a map of North America, Cape Breton Island looks out of position; that is, it is almost at right angles to the main peninsula of Nova Scotia. It certainly does look as if it were a separately floating chip which didn't apply the brakes soon enough. The geology of Cape Breton, although very similar to Nova Scotia, is just different enough to make the separate-chip theory tenable. Perhaps it was part of Scotland at one time or maybe Cornwall. It would be nice if it was, because so many Scots and Cornishmen came to Cape Breton to live. However, it isn't very important because once it arrived in its present position, it was subject to whatever geological influences were at work on the main land mass of North America.

Several times our island was buried, along with Nova Scotia, under huge glaciers, the result of the various ice ages which

2

ploughed off most of the mountains and the younger rocks right down to the basal granite.

It must have been a very different place before the first ice age, because from the way the basic rock tilts around Halifax, we believe that that part of Nova Scotia was a huge mountain—estimated to be over 20,000 feet high, which would have been clearly visible from Cape Breton. In fact, it is highly probable that Cape Breton was in the foothills of this huge mountain range.

All this has now gone and we can only try to imagine the scenery of that far-off time and the titanic force of the glaciers which could scrape away a 20,000-foot granite mountain leaving it flat and level.

Finally, the climate changed once more and the glaciers retreated again, leaving Cape Breton free of ice. This had a peculiar effect on the Island. The huge weight of ice had pressed the land downward into the sea of molten rock which is underneath the earth's crust, and once relieved of this weight the whole island started to rise. But it did not rise evenly. The northern part rose much faster than the southern part, so the island tilted.

If you draw a line from Capstick in the north to say Capelin Cove in the south, and you make a scale drawing of the land contours under that line, you will be able to place a straight edge over the hills and no hill will rise above it. That is, you can clearly see that it was once flat and level but has now tilted. If you do this accurately, you will immediately see the great valley, which is now the Bras d'Or Lakes, which in St. Andrews Channel is 981 feet below sea level.

There is no reasonable explanation at present for this pronounced tilt. Possibly the southern part is trapped under another plate, as the moving land masses are called. In the late 1800s, the redoubtable Hugh Fletcher noted that Louisbourg was sinking quite rapidly. In three years of close observation, he recorded a drop of over two feet

The pivot of the tilt appears to be north of Sydney, because Sydney Harbour is very much wider than it was 200 years ago. Forts constructed in 1720 are now underwater in the harbour. Sydney is sinking as well as Louisbourg, so it may well end up as a deepwater port. Fortunately, the rate at which Sydney is sinking appears to be slowing down, at least there is little indication of sinkage in recent years.

There was a very famous cartoon published in World War I. It showed the veteran "Ole Bill" sitting in the ruins of a building with a very new recruit. Above their heads was a huge shell-hole. "What made that hole?" asks the rookie. "Mice," says Ole Bill. I was reminded of this when I asked geologists how the Bras d'Or Lakes were formed, and received the reply, "Glaciers."

Let's consider this possibility. If you look at the map designed by the Cape Breton Development Corporation, which has shaded contours, you can easily trace the passage of the glaciers in the northern part of Cape Breton. Clearly the movement was north to south, and the same pattern is repeated along the south coast. The Bras d'Or Lakes equally clearly run from southwest to northeast.

If the Lakes were cut by the same glacier that formed the contours of the northern part, it must have made a U-turn. To make a glacier turn postulates that it met an immovable object. Remember that at Halifax a 20,000-foot granite mountain was brushed away by the glaciers—what is there more immovable than that? If there was such an object it would still be there, but there is no sign of anything unusual in the area. The Lakes could not have been cut by the same glacier that formed the north and south of the island.

Suppose the Lakes were already formed before this glacier passed over. This would mean that an unsupported bridge of ice over 20 miles long would have to pass over the Bras d'Or without sagging or breaking, since we have established that the last glaciation planed the Island flat. Such a happening is totally impossible. We are forced to the conclusion that the Bras d'Or was formed after the last glacier retreated.

Similarly it would be impossible to have purely local conditions of climate in an area of 100 miles by 60 miles, such that a small glacier could form and gouge out the lakes on its own, especially since it would have to occur during glacial retreat. It seems extremely unlikely that the standard answer, "Glaciers," can be true.

Subsidence also seems unlikely because the Big Bras d'Or

and St. Andrews channels are arrow-straight for more than 20 miles. Each cross several different types of rock formations which would have caused major turns, if it were subsidence. There has to be some other explanation.

I reached this point in the argument several years ago and was stuck until one day my youngest daughter, Stephanie, who was eight years old, made a remark which channeled my thoughts along new lines.

We had been talking about the Biblical version of Creation and how God made the Earth, when she asked, "What made God trip and fall on Cape Breton?" "What made you ask that?" I said. "Well, you can see where God put his right hand out to save himself from falling," she replied. Sure enough, the Lakes do resemble a right hand print. Lake Ainslie is the thumb, the eastern channels are the fingers and the southern lakes the palm print.

This set me thinking about something hitting the area from above, say a meteor. Years before, I had conducted a test program on mountings for aircraft electronics and we had fired special equipment into prepared trays of sand. When they broke up, various items flew off and produced tracks in the sand. Light items skimmed over the top, leaving shallow grooves, heavier items made deeper grooves and usually buried themselves. All the grooves could be seen to start from the same point, the point of impact.

If you take a map of Cape Breton and draw straight lines along the deepest parts of all the channels and include Lake Ainslie, Sydney Harbour, and the Mira, they all cluster together in the area of West Bay. Score one for the meteor theory.

It began to look as if a meteor could have come in at a low angle, striking in the area of West Bay, breaking into pieces which gouged out the channels. Some pieces bounced, producing Lake Ainslie, St. Ann's, Sydney Harbour, and the Mira.

Now the straight-line theory is good if the earth were stationary, but it isn't. It's rotating from west to east at something like 500 miles per hour at this latitude. You would only get straight lines under two conditions: if the object hitting the earth was travelling due east or west, or if it already was part of the earth and had the inertia and motion of the earth as part of its energy, for example, a bullet which travels in a straight line whichever direction you fire it.

If the object came from outer space and struck the earth rotating beneath it, we should see what is called the Coriolus effect. The Coriolus effect is seen in winds and ocean currents which are curved because of the Earth's rotation. Mathematically, it is the vector sum of the relative motions. More simply, something from outer space travelling from due south towards north and striking the earth will appear to turn towards the west if its speed and the speed of the earth's rotation are similar. The faster the speed of approach, the less turning will be observed, and vice versa.

From the sandbox experiments, we know that the heaviest pieces plow in deeply, slow more quickly and don't travel as far as the lighter bits which skitter across the surface. So if it was a meteor strike, we should seek evidence for the Coriolus effect in the deepest channel, which would be made by the biggest piece slowing down first.

You will need hydrographic charts with depth soundings to investigate this properly. Chart 4833 shows St. Andrews Channel to be the deepest, almost 1000 feet at its northern end. This huge gash is arrow-straight for nearly 20 miles until it reaches its deepest point—981 feet between Ironville and Long Island. Then—surprise, surprise, it turns northwards and westwards, a perfect Coriolus turn! Another point scored for the meteor.

If you can get hold of a geo-magnetic survey of Cape Breton, you will see that the "signature" of the older rocks to the north and south of the lakes is similar and quite pronounced, but in the lakes region it is weak and indefinite as if it had been disturbed. There is no sign of a big signature indicating the presence of the huge chunk of meteorite. I believe that this chunk is so deep it cannot give sizeable readings and the weak grouping on the geo-magnetic map at the head of the Coriolus turn is all we can detect of the huge mass. However, the grouping is there in the right place, and maybe someone will drill a deep hole one day and find the mass of iron or nickel or whatever remains. It is probably too deep to be recovered economically anyway.

Suppose the meteor theory is correct. Try to imagine what

must have happened on that fateful day. Sometime *within the period that man has been on Earth*, and probably 10,000 to 20,000 years ago, someone on the Pacific coast would have seen a bright star appear in the west. Moving at an incredible speed, it would have expanded in size and to unbearable brightness as it flashed overhead, its passage marked by peal after peal of thunder followed by hurricane-force winds. The watcher may have turned and watched terrified as the huge ball of rock, preceded by a mantle of incandescent air and trailing a tail of plasma and vaporized rock hundreds of miles long, streaked eastwards. If he were not blinded by the light or incinerated by the heat or crushed by the explosion of the super-heated air, he might have seen the broad swathe of forest under the meteor track burst into flame. Certainly by the time the meteor was over the eastern United States it would have caused widespread devastation due to the immense heat generated by its friction with the air.

The worst was yet to come and a deadly race had developed. The meteor was speeding across the surface of North America at probably thousands of miles per hour. Underneath, travelling a similar direction at a modest 500 m.p.h., the Earth was turning, carrying with it Cape Breton, at the easternmost tip of the continent. If the meteor had been only a few miles an hour faster, it would have missed Cape Breton, but it wasn't and it didn't. It struck and smashed. In a split second 160 cubic miles of Cape Breton were blasted to powder. One can only imagine what might have happened, for this is the biggest explosion in history. Krakatoa, which blew up with appalling violence in the nineteenth century, removed just over a cubic mile of material. Tens of thousands of people were drowned in the tidal waves which lasted for days, and the dust of Krakatoa did not settle for several years after being blasted into the stratosphere.

The Cape Breton meteor was 160 times worse. Tidal waves would have raced around the world, inundating the coasts. The immense amount of energy released by the impact in the form of heat would cause a mushroom cloud equivalent to thousands of H-bombs. Storms of appalling violence would have raged over the earth and the sky would be obscured by dust. Weeks after the impact, the sea entering the crater would have boiled, causing fogs mercifully hiding the destruction underneath.

Such a catastrophe would have affected the whole planet, and since it must have occurred during the period of homo sapiens—modern man—it is probable that some of the legends of floods and other terrible events may have their origin in Cape Breton. Certainly the legends of South America which tell how "the earth shuddered and groaned and the sky was darkened for months" seem to bear an echo of this terrible event, as do the many references to Lucifer, the fallen star.

David Dow was kind enough to let us publish this piece—originally a portion of a radio talk—with the understanding that we would present it as an unproven theory. Although based on some observation, Mr. Dow was not able to get corroboration on these ideas from scientists. We could have told you that at the start of this article, but we didn't want you to miss the experience of having the idea straight out and without reservations. The idea that the shape of Cape Breton was created out of the largest explosion the world has ever known is in itself appealing, and then to think that Cape Breton, in its extravagant formation, may have given birth to portions of several worldwide mythologies, is downright irresistible.

Map of Jacques Cartier's Second Voyage This map is a tracing from Bernard Hoffman's book *Cabot to Cartier*. The route is Cartier's second voyage, 1635 and 1636. The heavily outlined coasts are those descovered during this voyage. The coasts previously known are in lighter outline. Dotted coastline is unknown territory. We used modern names, retaining Hoffman's placement of Cape Lorraine.

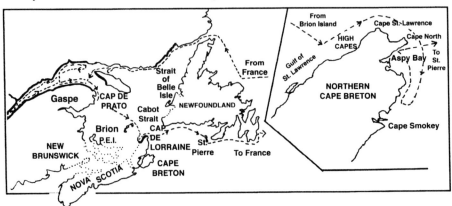

2

Jacques Cartier and Cape Breton's Shore

George Hermann

CARTIER WROTE one of the very first accounts of a portion of Cape Breton to appear in European history. But because the description of what he saw was submerged in his tale of more grand exploration and adventuring in Upper Canada, his depiction of our land has never been fully understood as a significant but entirely negative geographical discovery. In addition, he was the first to write of sailing from the Gulf of St. Lawrence to the Atlantic through the Cabot Strait, although he does not mention that Strait at all. Moreover, his account of Cape Breton, which ap-

pears towards the end of his relation of his second voyage, 1535-36, shows him to be a skillful and conscientious mariner, bold and cautious in turn, and mindful of the letter and the spirit of his duties to his king. Finally, we must keep foremost in our minds the distinction between the fact of discovery and the significance of that discovery. Cartier first saw the land of the Bretons and the Cabot Strait on his *homeward* voyage *to* France, but the significance of what he saw relates to outward voyaging *from* France, to a sailor coming in from a transatlantic voyage of 30 to 90 days duration, and bound for the new world of New France.

By the royal command of his king, François-premier, he had been directed, along with other duties, to perfect "the navigation of lands by you already begun, (and) to discover beyond les Terres Neufves." In doing so, Cartier described a cape of the land of the Bretons as "hauts a' merveille," wondrous high, to which he gave the name, Cape Lorraine. But where was it? What did he see there? Why was the cape important? When I read historians on this matter, I become confused because they cannot agree upon its location. I believe they misunderstand "the perfection of the navigation" set forth in Cartier's commission. Let us take Cartier's own accounts of his voyages and trace his route. We will find his accounts are clear and have only trivial errors.

The First Voyage

CARTIER MADE THREE VOYAGES to the New World under his king's commission, 1534, 1535-36, and 1541-42. His visit to Cape Breton took place on the second, but certain experiences and observations that he made on the first voyage were important for the second.

Cartier entered the Gulf on his first voyage by the strait between Labrador and the Newfoundland, the Strait of Belle Isle, at 51 1/2 degrees north, between June 15th and 19th, 1534 (New Style). This was quite early in the year, for passage of that strait (only 10 miles wide at its narrowest) is normally blocked with *drift* ice from the upper Gulf until July. Berg ice from the Atlantic is dangerous, but by itself would not prevent navigation. Early passage of the Strait (mid-June to early July) depends upon strong westerly winds to flush the drift ice into the Atlantic. The situation with respect to wind and drift ice is not unlike that in the Cabot Strait in the spring (April-May). The Cabot Strait allows entrance into the Gulf two months earlier than the Strait of Belle Isle.

After entering the Gulf Cartier made a circuit of it, sighting Cape Anguille on the southwestern corner of the Newfoundland on July 4th, and discovering Brion Island of the Madeleines [the Magdalen Islands] on July 5th, 1534. Brion lies 10 miles off the northern tip of the principal islands of the Madeleines. These islands are shaped like a long, slant letter "C" southwest to northeast, parallel to the Cape Breton shore. Here Cartier gives us our first clue to the location of Cape Lorraine. He observed the Madeleines:

About these islands there are high tides which set nearly southeast and northwest. I presume rather than otherwise, by what I have seen, that there may be another passage between New Land and the land of the Bretons. If so it were, it would be a great shortening as well of the *time* as of the *way*, if *perfection* be found in this voyage.

The key words are "time," "way," and "perfection." A southern passage to the Gulf (at 47 degrees north) would not be blocked with drift ice so late in the year as the Strait of Belle Isle. Moreover, the northern strait is on the latitude of Bristol, England. French seaports lie between 50 degrees and 44 degrees north. Thus, the southern passage might be a better one, easier for latitude sailing, besides being a shorter way.

Cartier did not take up the challenge of "the perfection of the navigation" on this voyage, for he had more important work to the westward. He reserved that problem for the future, and after reaching his furthermost west, Anticosti Island, he returned to France through the northern strait.

Tho Second Voyage

BY THE ROYAL COMMAND of his king, Cartier had been directed at the start of his second voyage, along with other duties, to perfect "the navigation of lands by you already begun." These are quite simple and clear orders. Because, if Cartier had found something valuable, his king would wish to know what was the best way by which to arrive. On his second voyage he put off the question of the southern passage, timing his entrance into the Strait of Belle Isle for mid-July to keep clear of the ice. Only after passing the winter of 1535-36 near the Rock of Quebec did Cartier consider "the perfection of the navigation" by considering the timing and the way of his own return to France. Furthermore, he might save the month of June by finding a southern passage.

He set off down the St. Lawrence River May 15th, 1536, with his two remaining ships, *La Grande Hermine* — about the size of a small dragger — and *L'Emerillon* — about the size of a longliner — and with his surviving mariners and gentlemen. Of May 30th he says:

And we made her go as far as athwart Cape Prato [Cape Percé], which is the beginning of the Bay Chaleur. And because the wind was good and convenient we stood on day and night, and the next day fetched the waist of the Isle of Brion [by Flagstaff Head] which we wished to do for to shorten our way. And the two lands are bearing southeast and northwest a quarter east and west; and it is fifty leagues [about 120 nautical miles] between them.

Between May 31st and June 4th, he explored the northern-most of the Madeleines. He says, "And Friday, the 4th, because the wind changed toward the coast (that is, toward Grosse Ile and Ile d'Est), we returned to the said Isle of Brion, where we were until the 10th of June."

This wind, I believe, was northwest or southeast, for he would not have lingered six more days at Brion had it been a fair, northwest wind. Moreover, he must have scrambled for the boats, for the wind and the sea rise quickly in this passage between Brion and the northernmost islands.

Early, perhaps before dawn on the 10th, having gotten his fair wind — which freshens considerably about 8 or 9 a.m. — he set a course somewhat to the south of southeast, "and went to fetch a high land, which lay to the southeast of the said island (of Brion), which appeared to us to be an island, and ranged it about twenty-two leagues and a half (52 nautical miles)."

On the way to this high land, he sailed along the eastern

shore of the Madeleines of which he saw three islands that lay toward the sands, which, he says, were likewise an island. After leaving the Madeleines, he closed with the shore of a high land, and sailed some distance beyond the cape that he would later call Lorraine. He then concluded the "high and level land" was not an island but was mainland, "...and the said land, which is high and level land, to be the mainland falling off to the northwest [southwest]. After which things were known we returned to the cape of the said land [Cape Lorraine]."

This was a long sail for a day. Not only did he sail from Brion to the "high and level" land of the Bretons, some 60 or 65 nautical miles, but he coasted Cape Breton for over 35 to 40. The total nearly equals his sail from Cape Prato to Brion of May 30-31. I suppose it was nearly nightfall before he tucked his vessels under the windward shore, the south side of Cape Lorraine.

If I accept Cape North, for the moment, as Cape Lorraine, I can reasonably imagine that he fell in with the Cape Breton shore somewhere between MacKenzie Point and the High Capes. Then he rounded Cape St. Lawrence—which he might not have seen, for it is nearly invisible against the high land behind it, being but 50 feet above the sea. Then he turned Cape North and coasted somewhat beyond White Point to conclude, by observing Cape Smokey to the southwest, that he had fetched mainland. Then he returned to Cape North.

There can be no doubt Cartier knew himself to be in Atlantic water, for his next course was set for the Newfoundland.

By nightfall of the 10th, Cartier had found his passage between "New Land and the land of the Bretons" and also had found a monumental cape to mark its western shore—for Cape North is the *only* high cape within reasonable sailing from Brion in a day, near to which an experienced mariner could shelter the king's two vessels for three nights. Smokey is too far. Chéticamp is off course and does not mark a passage. Moreover, Cape North is truly monumental, being visible from the sea long before any other cape such as St. Lawrence or White Point or Long Point or St. Paul Island. Cape North makes a fine seamark. I have no doubt he lay that night to the south of the Cape, perhaps near Sperling

Brook, for the descriptions that we will shortly read are all of the Atlantic side of Cape North.

But was this a better passage than the northern one? Cartier could not know until he searched Aspy Bay for a good haven—a harbour into which the voyager from France could find safety, water, wood, seafowl, and could give thanks for his safe voyage across the hazardous Atlantic. Cape Lorraine (Cape North) was to be a seamark for the *inbound* sailor to New France, as Brion was one for the *outbound* sailor to Old France.

Now the morning watch of June 11th would be treated—as countless codfishermen, lobstermen, swordfishermen after him would be so treated—to the brave sight of the pink and yellow dawn flooding in from the sea and the great sun rising up from under the sea, its rays lighting up the red granite side of Cape Lorraine, striking along the high-cliffed scarp far to the westward, dissolving the smoky mists of the North and South Ponds, shining down upon the sandy bars and white gypsum cliffs, brightening the somber hardwood greens of the lowland valley behind those bars, and making the surf flash off White Point.

Cartier spent the next two days exploring Aspy Bay. Aspy Bay has eroded since Cartier's time from a gentle arc stretching from the Merry Pisser to Black Head—the soft-rock lowland—and the process is continuing. Here is what Cartier reports of the Bay and Cape Lorraine:

...which forms itself into two or three capes wondrous high, and a great depth of water, and the tide so swift that more is not possible. We named this cape Cape Lorraine, which is forty-six degrees and a half, to the south of which cape there is a lowland and seemingly some river entrance, but there is no harbour of worth. Above which lands toward the south lies another headland, which we named Cape St. Paul, which is in forty-seven degrees and a quarter [actually, 46 1/4].

The awe that Cape North strikes in its seaborne beholder is reflected in the first three clauses of the narrative: the cape is "hauts a' merveille," the sea is "grand profond," the tide such that "qu'il n'est possible de plus." There is no other cape, I should say, below Cape St. John on the Atlantic shore of the Newfoundland, upon which such superlatives may, with justice, be thrust.

Jacques Cartier and Cape Breton's Shore

Cape North is over 1400 feet at its highest. It is composed of a pink granite which has a bright red appearance where it is scoured by the waves. It has at its extremity two points, Cape North and Money Point. If lower Cape Breton is a clenched fist, Cape North is a finger pointing to Newfoundland. The 30 and 60 fathom sounding are close inshore. Shallower water (marking the entrance to the Bay) begins on a line roughly from Money Point to White Point. Finally, the current from the Gulf, the Atlantic tides, and the stout winds all make for a rough sea. Rip tides are common. A lop tide forms under the southeast wind off Money Point which sets up great pyramidal waves through which a fisherman travels with caution.

The fact that Cartier found no harbour of worth and that he quite likely found anchorage difficult leads me to conclude he was uneasy, kept an eye on the wind, and was anxious to be off. Nevertheless, he searched the Bay two days, for he tells us of the lowland forming the Sunrise Valley and the presence of a river for fresh water (probably the North Aspy). He took the latitude the next noon and was in error by nearly one-half degree too low. Perhaps he sent *L'Emerillon* off White Point to view Smokey (his Cape St. Paul) from outside Long Point (also called Cape Egmont). Smokey is exactly one-quarter of a degree "above and to the south" of White Point. The 47 1/4 degrees of the manuscript should read 46 1/4. Smokey is also visible over the top of South Mountain from the modern tower atop Money Point, but there is no indication Cartier sent a party to climb the cape.

All this summed was Cartier's disappointment. "There is no harbour of worth." Without a safe harbour—though water, wood, and seafowl were abundant—Aspy Bay could be no haven for the transatlantic sailor. It was open to the winds from the northeast through the southeast. Unless a convenient haven in Newfoundland could be found, this wondrous high cape with its red granite wall would not mark a more perfect navigation to New France. Cartier did not find such a harbour in Newfoundland. Therefore, on his third voyage to the New World, Cartier again used the northern strait, the Strait of Belle Isle, both coming and going.

Yet those red cliffs he had seen were surely red enough to

rouge a Cardinal's cape — red enough for one such of the House of Guise-Lorraine — and thus he named this red cape, Lorraine, for a churchman of that house. And he set off for the Newfoundland:

> Sunday, the 13th day of the said month, the day and feast of Pentecost, we had knowledge of the east-southeast of New Land, which was about twenty-two [32?] leagues from the said cape, and because the wind was contrary we made for a harbour, which we named the harbour of St. Esperit, until Tuesday, when we got under way from the said harbour and ranged the said coast as far as to the Isles of St. Pierre.

Why North Is Down

BEFORE MAPS AND COMPASS directions were generally in use, directions were taken from the flow of current along a shore. "Above" was where the current came from. "Below," where it went. "Up" and "down," the same. In Red River people would speak, for example, of going "up to Chéticamp" or "down to the Lower End," or that "Chéticamp is *above* Pleasant Bay." In these terms, Cape North is the down-most cape in Cape Breton. Likewise, the use is capable of some generalization. One goes "up to Boston" or "up to New York." One goes "down to the Newfoundland" or "down to the Labrador." Upper and Lower Canada are so described by the meaning of this usage, with the flow of the Great River of Canada (the St. Lawrence) as the datum. Since rivers on the Atlantic shore of North America generally flow from west to east, the Maritime Provinces and the Boston States were traditionally known as "Down East." When one is in Bonne Bay in Newfoundland, there is a problem, solved by common sense. One goes "down the shore to the Cabot Strait" and one also goes "down the shore to the Strait of Belle Isle." One never goes up to anywhere from Bonne Bay.

With respect to this usage, Cartier is perfectly consistent and clear when he describes Cape St. Paul as being "above and to the south" of Cape Lorraine. Conversely, the location of Cape Lorraine is then perfectly clear. It is below and to the north of Cape Smokey. Only Cape North can fit that description.

George Hermann taught high school mathematics in New York City. He spent his summers in a three-walled building at the Lower End, north of Pleasant Bay, Inverness County–looking out to the Atlantic, reading, walking the woods. One autumn he decided not to go back to New York. He built the fourth wall and lived out the rest of his life in Cape Breton.

3

Irish Convicts Abandoned in Cape Breton, 1788

Charles A. Burke

O N THE AFTERNOON OF DECEMBER 11, 1788, a ship landed Irish convicts on a desolate, uninhabited beach in eastern Cape Breton. The captain's mission was simple enough. Without food, proper clothing, or local assistance, he hoped most would perish in hours. Circumstances proved otherwise, however, and by August 1789, a soldier in the 42nd Regiment wrote from Sydney:

I must not forget to tell you that the Master of a vessel from Dublin not thinking there were rascals enough upon the Island, thought proper to land 60 male and 18 female convicts upon the coast and left them to pick out their

road the best way they could[.] [T]he consequence was that seven of them died immediately from the severity of the weather.... Two of them have since been hanged for robbery; two more under sentence of death for murder, seven in Prison to take their trials before the court...and the remainder are travelling about the country at large to improve the morals of the people[.] One is comforted however from the reflection that the danger of their being corrupted is not great.[1] [Notes are on page 166.]

The survivors of this ill-fated voyage were the last convicts Britain allowed to remain in her North American colonies. Their arrival that December afternoon ended a century-old transportation system that by 1775 had become a major ingredient of English criminal law.[2] Convicts represented a quarter of all British emigrants to America during the eighteenth century: 36,000 English, 13,000 Irish, 700 Scottish.[3] After African slaves, they made up the largest group of forced immigrants to North America.[4]

Although Britain transported most convicts for non-capital crimes, many had committed serious offenses. Non-capital charges ranged from possession of stolen goods to bigamy, assault with intent to rob, manslaughter, and the most frequent charge, grand larceny.[5] In Ireland, vagrancy was associated with petty crime, begging, and prostitution, and they banished vagrants in great numbers.[6] Through transportation and banishment, they saved hundreds of felons from the gallows. By 1773, many considered transportation the "most humane and effectual Punishment [in Britain]."[7]

The average convict was indigent and without opportunity long before banishment. The typical transport was a young, unskilled male, from the lower socioeconomic class. Although most were "driven to crime out of economic hardship, many had also committed reasonably serious offenses, in some cases [repeatedly]."[8] The courts often laid easily proven charges against habitual criminals as an expedient method to ensure quick transport.

After young men, women were the second staple of the convict trade. Although generally called prostitutes, it is certain that they transported no women for the crime because it was never a transportable offence. The courts banished female convicts for theft, usually of a petty sort, with crimes of violence figuring low.

Irish Convicts Abandoned in Cape Breton, 1788

When the American colonies refused entry to British ships in 1775, they limited Britain's ability to transport convicts and triggered a crisis in the criminal justice system. Britain enacted the Hulks Act in 1776—a measure designed to house convicts aboard abandoned warships moored in the Thames and at Plymouth and Portsmouth. Despite this, the convict population in Provincial jails swelled by 73% in the decade after 1776.[9] The decade witnesses a soaring crime rate as well, with increased dependence on capital punishment. In 1782, the courts executed nearly 100 felons in London and Middlesex, and the upsurge in hangings throughout England convinced public officials of the need to renew convict transportation.

After much debate, Parliament enacted a new transportation act in 1784. They could not agree on a destination for felons, however, opposing plans to ship convicts in 1785 to Africa and to Canada and the West Indies in 1786. They settled finally on New South Wales, Australia, in 1786. Meanwhile, the Irish Act of 1786 authorized the Lord Lieutenant of Ireland to transport convicts to any of his Majesty's plantations or settlements in America or to any place outside Europe.[10] The Irish Parliament voted to send convicts to Botany Bay, Australia, in 1790.

The government selected Botany Bay for several reasons—each reason more significant than as a dumping site for convicts. First, it supported Britain's claim to Australia and prevented French or Dutch settlement. Second, it provided a new trade route to China in case a French-Dutch alliance closed the East Indies route.[11] Third, a colony in Botany Bay could provide naval resources for the eastern fleet, be self-sufficient in wartime, and provide sanctuary from French, Dutch, and Spanish bases in the area. As one scholar recently claimed, the choice of New South Wales served many motives but "the removal of the convicts from the realm was secondary—an accompaniment, but not a cause."[12]

Meanwhile, removal of convicts from the realm was the prime reason for a ship loading Irish prisoners at Dublin on Saturday morning, October 18, 1788. Captain Debonham, master of the snow *Providence* from North Yarmouth, England, contracted to carry 126 convicts from Dublin and Cork to Nova Scotia. The *Freeman's Journal* reported:

> All the criminals under the rule of transportation were brought from the New Prison. There were no less than 14 cartloads of men; the large vehicles which carried the prisoners from the gaol to the Court was loaded with unfortunate females [as well].... This precious cargo is taken in for Nova Scotia and the Captain of the vessel is bound under severe penalty to land them all at the place of destination.[13]

Although Cape Breton sources are few, the Dublin newspapers provide some detail. The *Freeman's Journal* recorded:

> Among the prisoners now confined in the Newjail there are a considerable number of idle women committed by the divisional justices of police as vagrants of infamous character, who nightly infested the streets of this metropolis at unseasonable hours for the purposes of robbery or prostitution and having no honest means of livelihood.[14]

A further description of the prisoners offered shortly after their departure noted:

> Among the transports sent off last Saturday morning, amounting to upwards of 140 male and females, there were several of the most daring and desperate lawless ruffians, as well as of the most infamous and abandoned prostitutes with which this metropolis...had been infested. The ridding of the city of these dangerous pests must greatly contribute to the establishment of public peace and personal security.[15]

Although many of their names and crimes remain unknown, identifying most of the convicts transported to Cape Breton that fall is possible. Among the lists were Elizabeth Jones, transported for seven years for theft of three silver tablespoons and several pieces of plate; John Hart, banished seven years for the theft of four pounds of brass; Michael Hutchison, seven years for cow and sheep stealing; fourteen-year-old Michael Reddy, seven years for theft of a silver spoon; Richard Corrigan, theft of a watch; John and Henry Walsh sentenced to transport for the "theft of a ladder with intent to use for more theft"; and Judith Butler, Rose Reilly, Ann Lynch and many other women convicted of vagrancy and transported for seven years.

Aboard the *Providence*, as on all convict ships, they chained prisoners below decks in damp, unlit quarters. During the voyage they experienced seasickness, dysentery, and possibly smallpox or typhus. These diseases often claimed 1/3 of many convict transports and the *Providence* was no exception; 46 (37%) died on the crossing. The quality of shipboard food and water was poor as well. A historical compilation suggests a convict consumed a weekly diet of 1.2 pounds of beef and pork, 13.3 ounces of cheese, 4.7 pounds of bread, half a quart of peas, 1.7 quarts of oatmeal, 1.3 ounces of molasses, half a gill of gin, and 5.3 gallons of water.[16]

The pitiful shipboard conditions, however, were the least of a convict's worries. Since the American War, several Irish transports to North America ended in barbarous circumstances. When the Brig *Nancy* ran short of food in 1784, the captain landed 46 prisoners illegally on the Spanish Island of Ferro. Soldiers immediately surrounded the convicts and put them to death. A 1785 voyage sold 176 convicts as indented servants in Maryland. A third ship carried 190 prisoners to indentured servitude in Alexandria, Virginia. The fourth vessel, the snow *Dispatch*:

> of Yarmouth, Captain Nappers, sailed in June 1787 and took 183 convicts.... They landed them at the new Loyalist settlement of Shelburne, in Nova Scotia[,] but the people there would not suffer them to land and in consequence the Captain was induced to put them ashore in a remote unsettled part of the bay of Machias [Maine, US], from whence the survivors begged their way into the more southern and different parts of the US saying they were indented servants from Ireland who had been put on shore from suffering a want of provisions and water on ship-board.[17]

The fifth vessel sailed from Dublin with 100 convicts in 1787. When the master landed them on a deserted Bahamian Island, the convicts endured months of incredible deprivation during which fifty-one persons died. The Captain who rescued the survivors reported "the living were eating the carcasses of the dead."[18]

CHAINED BELOW DECK in the *Providence*, convicts knew the fate of previous voyages. After seven weeks crossing the wintry Atlantic, their ship finally reached northeastern Cape Breton. Observing the snow-covered ground and fearful of delaying his return trip, Captain Debonham resolved to abandon his cargo at once. Planning to return through the Strait of Canso, Debonham sought to abandon the convicts at a remote, uninhabited headland, far from authority.

Late in the afternoon of December 11, Captain Debonham anchored the *Providence* opposite the windswept shoreline between Port Nova Island and Scatarie. Bringing the prisoners on deck, Debonham's crew removed their leg irons and forced them into the ship's yawl. According to a deposition made by Francis Dixon, Chief Pilot of Mainadieu, Debonham's seamen:

> were armed with Pistols, cutlasses and swords & when the Boat reached shore, they tumbled [the convicts] headlong from the boat into the surf...and one man was killed by being thrown against a rock.[19]

The yawl made six or seven trips that afternoon, landing the eighty men, women, and boys at several locations on the coast now known as Convict Point. By 7:00 p.m., Captain Debonham was free of his charges and the *Providence* hoisted sail to the west.

The convicts were left to endure a night that Francis Dixon said was "excessively cold...the ground covered with snow."[20] They huddled in small groups, disoriented, their clothes soaked from the landing—many without stockings and shoes, and all without food or blankets. Six convicts perished of exposure that night. One old man, John Kirkpatrick, was beaten, robbed, and left to die by two of his convict mates, Joseph MacDonald and Laurence Pendergast.

The Irish newspapers document some of Pendergast's career in crime. Earlier in the year he served time in Newgate for forging a bill of exchange. Law courts knew him as an old offender with previous convictions in Drogheda and Trim for passing forged notes. In September, the Dublin court convicted him of two more highway robberies and banished him for seven years. They tried and convicted MacDonald, his murderous accomplice, for several felonies only days before the *Providence* sailed. The courts banished Kirkpatrick, the poor victim, for life for sheep stealing.[21]

Many others might have perished as well but for the good fortune that Charles Martell was cutting firewood nearby. Martell, the King's Justice of the Peace in Mainadieu, a respected colonist, and retired soldier from Wolfe's army at Louisbourg, encountered one group of convicts who related their plight. He brought them to Mainadieu at once, where, he later told the governor, the residents provided "what assistance they could without injuring their own families."[22] Later that evening, Martell and Francis Dixon organized a search for the remaining convicts, finding another thirty or forty. At a December 15 Council meeting Dixon told the Lieutenant Governor that when they found the convicts "the greatest part of them [were] little better than naked."[23]

Over the next three days, the villagers of Mainadieu cared for the convicts. On the 15th they loaded 40 convicts, all the females and those suffering frostbite, aboard Luke Keegan's fishing boat the *Shilaly*, bound for Sydney.

The inauspicious arrival of destitute persons in Cape Breton that winter raised immediate alarm. Although the population of Sydney only doubled the convict number, Sydney's merchants had barely enough provisions to last until spring. In addition, the Lieutenant-Governor, William Macarmick, was unable to cover new expenses, having spent the contingency funds earlier during the visit of Prince William Henry, later King William IV. Furthermore, several merchants remained unpaid for excessive bills run up by J. F. W. DesBarres, the island's previous administrator.

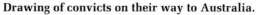

Drawing of convicts on their way to Australia.

Learning of the convicts' arrival, Macarmick ordered Keegan's ship to dock at the military wharf with a guard to prevent them from landing. He then called an emergency Council meeting, advising the senior merchant, Keith Stout, to feed and clothe the convicts. The next day, Council met with Sydney's merchants to determine the quantity of provisions on hand. Discovering that supplies hardly met local requirements, Council voted to ship some convicts to Halifax aboard the Treasury brig *Relief* with the rest to follow in hired vessels.

On December 19, Council informed Macarmick they could induce no vessel to risk a voyage and the *Relief*'s captain refused to sail with more than ten or twelve convicts. Faced with quartering the convicts until spring, Council advised Macarmick to learn what supplies were available and to request instructions from the Secretary of State, Lord Sydney. Macarmick rented a large house at once, lodged the convicts and placed them under a military guard. Later that day he wrote to Lord Grenville, the Home Secretary:

> whatever their destination was, or whatever their crimes...may have been, they came to me in so miserable a state and by an Act so cruel, that were they not H.M.'s Subjects I could not resist the pressing Inducements to give them protection.[24]

The following day Macarmick solicited advice from the Colonial Secretary and requested an immediate shipment of supplies from Governor Parr in Halifax. He shipped the letters aboard the brig *Relief* but in a bizarre turn of events, a storm blew the ship off course, and the master, later claiming insanity, sailed to the West Indies where he remained until May.[25] This incident prevented the delivery of Macarmick's letters, with the consequence that neither Halifax nor London was aware of the precarious situation in Cape Breton. Without direction, Macarmick was forced to support the convicts from his own meager Treasury.

References to the convicts over the next few months are scant. As winter continued, fifteen to sixteen convicts remained in the hospital recovering from frostbite received that first night in the woods. Several were permanently lamed and others died of the exposure. Rev. Ranna Cossit of St. George's Anglican

Church notes in his Vestry Book the deaths of several: "Buried Woodhousen, one of the convicts, 23rd Dec. 1788.... Patrick Doyl, one of the convicts, Buried 2nd Jan. 1789."

In March 1789, many soldiers guarding the convicts became ill and the surgeon of the 42nd Regiment reported to Macarmick that "some infectious disorder might have been brought among [the convicts'] rags."[26] Macarmick ordered the convicts to a quarantine house about seven miles from Sydney and their clothing destroyed. Describing the event to Lord Sydney, Macarmick wrote:

The severity of the Weather rendered the removal of these miserable people a measure of much difficulty; one Woman died, and one Man has since been frozen to death...carrying provisions for the others.[27]

When Council learned the disease originated elsewhere they returned the convicts to Sydney. Although many returned to guarded quarters, some were free to explore the community. Writing to Secretary Grenville, Provost Marshall David Taitt complained of the convict women who were found "rioting at a Public House of bad fame,"[28] and it is likely the convict charged with murder that March committed the crime while free.

Shortly after the contagion alarm, the capital of Cape Breton watched the trial of Pendergast and MacDonald with interest. Accused of murdering Fitzpatrick the first night ashore, the Grand Jury found both guilty and sentenced them to be hanged on March 14, 1789. However, Governor Macarmick ordered a stay of execution. Since the authorities did not recover Kirkpatrick's body, Macarmick wondered how the jury could be certain that death resulted from the beating and not from exposure. As the Attorney General noted, evidence against the accused from other convicts might not be "entirely purged of malice growing out of former animosities."[29] Council sought Grenville's advice, but meanwhile Pendergast and MacDonald escaped and were not heard from again.

Writing to Lord Sydney in May 1789, Macarmick reported the convicts:

remain a heavy burthen upon Government, and the poverty and fewness of the Inhabitants prevent their being employed to any advantage. I have determined to take hold of the first and best opportunity to get rid of them.[30]

In other words, he was letting them go where they pleased. By late spring, Macarmick freed all convicts not facing current charges. Later that year, Home Secretary Grenville referred to the convicts employed in Cape Breton as "no longer a Burthen on the public." By October 1789, Macarmick advised Grenville the convicts were all gone, except for two held in jail on a charge of murder. These two escaped in April 1790, were recaptured, and pardoned in December.[31]

Informing the Lord Lieutenant of Ireland of the convicts' plight in Cape Breton, Home Secretary Grenville wrote July 27, 1789:

This transaction appears to have been attended with circumstances of so atrocious a nature that...measures should be taken to recover from the Master of the vessel the penalties of the Bonds which he is required by Law to give.[32]

Grenville advised him further that:

the transportation of Convicts to His Majesty's Colonies in North America is in many respects so objectionable...[that] by the Act of the 26th of His present Majesty, You are not to direct or authorize the Transportation of Offenders to the Colonies...or to any other part of His Majesty's Dominions [other] than the Coast of New South Wales.[33]

These instructions were a direct result of Captain Debonham's brutal act on the coast of Cape Breton seven months earlier, and ended the practice of convict transportation to North America.

George Moore, Esq., an Irishman and naval officer in Sydney, echoed the sentiments of the Home Secretary in a letter published in a Dublin newspaper the same month. He wrote:

Eighty miserable wretches (our compatriots) landed [here]...at the distance of twelve miles from any inhabited place; some drowned in the landing, and many [were] frostbitten before they could receive any assistance. Surely humanity must shudder at the manner in which convicts are disposed of and to remedy this evil is certainly a measure highly deserving the interference of the legislature. [To which the editor added] that such ill-fated wretches [were better]...hanged at home, sooner than face the lingering death of famine in the inclement wilds of America.[34]

In the end, the convicts went their separate ways, drawn to places by opportunity or circumstance. Of the 126 Irish men, women, and boys who boarded the *Providence* that October 18, 1788, 46 died crossing the Atlantic, one man was killed during the landing, six died of exposure the first night, and one was murdered. In the following months three died in hospital, one woman died en route to the hospital and one man froze to death carrying supplies.

Little is known about the remaining sixty-seven convicts. Two murderers escaped from prison and disappeared. The government reprieved two other murderers. A report from April 1789 noted that some convicts were seen "lurking about Halifax," and we know that Luke Keegan of Mainadieu kept a young boy as a servant.[35] Although we assume the authorities brought the remaining twenty convicts from Mainadieu to Sydney, there is no record of this event. In all likelihood, the local population absorbed some convicts as servants and settlers. The Home Secretary Lord Grenville admits as much in October 1789 when he refers to the "convicts employed in Cape Breton as no longer a Burthen on the public."[36]

The British Treasury eventually paid £567 for the support and maintenance of the convicts, about £60 less than Captain Debonham received to transport them in the first place. Despite Grenville's petition, the Irish authorities failed to punish the captain for his callous abandoning of the convicts on a desolate headland.

Inasmuch as Captain Debonham planned to avoid discovery or notoriety, his action that December afternoon led to a major shift in British foreign policy, the naming of Cape Breton's "Convict Point," and the tale's passage into our oral tradition.

Charles A. Burke delivered "Irish Convict Transportation to Cape Breton, 1788" as a talk at the Irish Cultural Symposium in Louisbourg, August 1995; and, with additions, the Old Sydney Society, March 1997, called "Rascals Enough Upon the Island." He published a reviced text in *Cape Breton's Magazine*, Number 72, June 1997, and then a new version in *The Nashwaak Review*, Volume 22/23, Number 1 Spring/Summer 2009.

Mr. Burke is an archeologist in the national park system. He reminds us that the Irish convict trade used the same captains and ships as the slave trade to Ghana. He first heard the story of Irish convicts in Cape Breton from his father's uncles in Baleine.

The drawing of convicts on their way to Australia, and the list of crimes punishable by transportation, were found on the Internet.

Crimes for Which People Were Transported

Denominated Single Felonies: punishable by Transportation, Whipping, Imprisonment, the Pillory, and Hard Labour in Houses of Correction, according to the nature of the offence. The principal of which are the following: Grand Larceny, which comprehends every species of Theft above the value of One Shilling not otherwise distinguished. Receiving or buying stolen goods, Jewels and Plate. Ripping and stealing Lead, Iron, Copper, &c. Or buying or receiving. Stealing (or receiving when stolen) Ore from Black Lead Mines. Stealing from Furnished lodgings. Setting fire to underwood. Stealing Letters or destroying a Letter or Packet advancing the Postage, and secreting the Money. Embezzling Naval Stores, in certain cases. Petty Larcenies or Thefts under One Shilling. Assaulting with an intent to Rob. Aliens returning after being ordered out of the kingdom. Stealing fish from a Pond or river—Fishing in inclosed ponds, and buying stolen Fish. Stealing Roots, Trees, or plants, of the value of 5s. Or destroying them. Stealing Children with their apparel. Bigamy, or Marrying more Wives or Husbands than one. Assaulting and Cutting, or Burning Clothes. Counterfeiting the Copper Coin &c. Marriage solemnizing clandestinely. Manslaughter, or killing another without Malice, &c... Cutting or Stealing Timber Trees, &c. Stealing a Shroud out of a Grave.

4

Fr. Jimmy Tompkins Speaking, 1938

THE ANTIGONISH MOVEMENT is Adult Education. In forecasting its future, we must necessarily go into the content of Adult Education. We might ask ourselves, "What is its subject matter? What is its scope? Where is it most needed?"

We all now believe that Education is co-extensive and co-terminous with life. There are no zones of human activity closed to the human mind. In whatever sphere of human experience, wherein there are unrequited needs of man, *there* is the *ministry* of the mind and the spirit. Adult Education is not limited to the multiplication table. It takes into account man as a spiritual being, it seeks to establish just relationships as between man and man in the economic order. It examines the mutual problems of producer and consumer.

We are not so much concerned with setting the yard limits of Adult Education as we are with throwing the switches which will give the average man unobstructed passage to wider fields of knowledge, self-help and security, and let him find his own way.

Beware of Institutionalizing

IF THERE IS ONE WARNING, it is this—beware of institutionalizing. I can illustrate best what I mean by relating a story which they tell in New York about Lincoln Steffens. It is told of Mr. Steffens that he was one day walking down Broadway with the devil. They saw an ideal floating in the air. A passerby seized the ideal and put it in his pocket. Mr. Steffens said to the devil, "That is going to be bad for your business, isn't it?"

"Oh, no," said the devil, "I'll teach him to organize it."

When a thing becomes over-institutionalized, it tends to become sterile. It seems to me that that is what has happened to formal education. We might well ask ourselves if something similar has not happened to those religious people who sit back, at times like these, when so many millions have become propertyless, stricken with fear of economic insecurity, homeless waifs of a hit-and-miss industrialism.

It is this kind of thing that enables severe critics of Christianity to say that religion is the opiate of the people. It is *not* Christianity that is the opiate of the people, it is the inert state of Christians that furnishes some semblance of truth to this libel. *It is fossilized education that is the opiate of the people.* It keeps them from getting the truth about the condition that they are in. Says Douglas Gerrold in his "Future of Freedom": "On hearing of the adoption in all civilized countries of compulsory education, the inhabitant of Mars would assume a wide diffusion of culture, the exaction by an educated electorate of new standards of logic from publicists, and of new standards of enlightenment from statesmen.... He would feel assured that means at last exist for bringing home to all classes, by the most direct and effective of methods, the facts of every problem, means for breaking up class or sectional or national prejudice and for combating and conquering ignorance."

In every one of these anticipations, the inhabitant of Mars would be wholly wrong. The problems of ignorance, of irreligion, of class prejudice, of national, racial and class hatred which were visible on the surface of things a hundred years ago, have today struck roots so deep and so powerful that they threaten the very foundations of our civilization.... Meanwhile, envy, born of *ignorance* and fed by *material greed*, threatens to destroy society from within.

Adult Education for Everyone

ADULT EDUCATION IS NOT FOR ILLITERATES alone nor is it to pap-feed social climbers with appreciations of Shakespeare and Beethoven. It should be designed for the best brains we have, to wrestle with the worst problems we have — want and frustrated lives literally crushed under a heritage of plenty which these people cannot get their hands on....

Not only must it be prepared to accept *truth* where it finds it, it must also be prepared to accept *talent* where it finds it. Our experience in the Antigonish Movement is that there is more real Adult Education at the pit-heads, down in the mines, out among the fishermen's shacks, along the wharves, and wherever the farmers gather to sit and talk in the evenings, than you can get from one hundred thousand dollars worth of fossilized formal courses. It springs from the hearts and pains of the people. It is spontaneous — call it the cracker-barrel type, if you will — I vote for the cracker-barrel. The former doesn't fill any empty pantry, it doesn't bring milk and food and health back to babies blighted with malnutrition already in their toddling years. We want *ideas* with *marrow* in them.

It may be said by oracles of the opiate school of education — those peddlers of dope and drugs in the realm of ideas — that education, such as I am talking about, smacks of propaganda. Well, what of it? Would you accuse a man, looking for a place to sleep for the night, of propaganda? If so, we are propagandists.

If education is not the propaganda of truth, then it is not education....

Adult Education is the knowledge that ministers to self-development, character and social intelligence. I see no reason why, using your brains to bring knowledge, that is, power, to bear upon something that will put necessities on your bare table, clothes on your naked back and a covering over your head, should be called propaganda.

It is technically impossible anyhow to keep people in ignorance today concerning economic affairs. It has become technically impossible — quite apart from the ethics of the thing — to keep people in the dark about who gets the lion's share of the wealth that issues out of the economic processes. There are too many ways of getting "wised up."

Libraries Promote Adult Education

THE CHIEF INSTRUMENT for promoting Adult Education will be the well-stocked Regional Library, the people's university of the future, supported as our public schools are.

It will not emphasize alone books, but interpreters of books and trained guides in the choice of books and subjects, suitable to the needs and tastes of the reader.

The trained librarian of the Regional Library ought to be, first and foremost, an Adult Educator. It is one thing to be active in library service and it may be quite another thing to be a promoter of Adult Education. Adult Education works towards the development of the community. A library might unwittingly become a hindrance rather than a help in the spread of genuine education — Adult or otherwise — and become like so much formal education in the past, *the opiate of the people*.

The American Association of Adult Education feels that one of its chief duties today is to set men "free from the utter drabness of unfulfilled lives." To do this, our methods must be flexible and informal. Faith in the educatability of the average man is one of the chief underlying ideas of the Antigonish Movement.

Today, we tremble before the spectre of war. Enthusiasm can

be whipped up by militarists. Why not the same enthusiasm for feeding and clothing people as there is for killing them? We are not against propaganda on these occasions, are we? If we co-operate for death, we ought to be able to co-operate for life. People in times of crisis have to be shocked into knowing the true nature of things. People have, for too long, been fooled into hiding their light under a bushel, largely by propaganda, for laissez-faire and in the interests of greed.

Religion, Education and Economics

IN REGARD TO THE FUTURE, I am not so concerned with setting the exact limits of the Antigonish Movement. This education is not confined to economic things alone. For 150 years, we have been listening to the propaganda—keep religion out of business. The fact is that laissez-faire industrialism is reeking with religion—the cult of fatalism that expects things of themselves to come out from around the corner. And the peculiar thing about this *negative* religion is that it follows the machine all over the world and has become the week-day religion of people, no matter at what altar they may worship on Sunday. It was, and it is, a cult most convenient to the upholders of laissez-faire. Interference by governments or organizations of any kind were decried as taboo on the ground of being artificial, by the liberalistic junta, which, in the name of liberty, found license to rob and ruthlessly exploit. The Sermon on the Mount was fine for Sundays but had no place on weekdays.

When we suggest the various possible fields of Adult Education, this, to my mind, is one of them that can be explored by the multitude whose oxen have been gored for the last 150 years. To me this seems a very proper subject for Adult Education.... The main thing is that it will be done.... The program of the Antigonish Movement is broad enough and big enough to take in right thinking men of all creeds who are awakened to the gravity of the social conditions today, and who have felt the desire to do something. Such men belong to many divisions of the Christian religion, and include many who do not profess to be Christians. After all, what we are all looking for, is a world where men can live.

It may be, then, the unique destiny of the Adult Education Movement to bridge the breach between religion and economics — as modern research is bridging the breach between religion and science.

Fr. Jimmy Tompkins called this article "The Future of the Antigonish Movement." He is considerd the spiritual father of the Antigonish Movement, though actually he was a daring firebrand and extremely down-to-earth fighter for social justice. See the biography by Jim Lotz and Michael R. Welton called *Father Jimmy*.

An example of adult education and cooperation: A Study Club meeting of Ray MacNab, John Allan Smith, Duncan Currie, Angus Currie and Mary Arnold, a co-operator who came to Reserve Mines, Cape Breton, to share her experiences. Joe Laben told us that each man and his wife built these little houses out of cardboard, built them to scale, and that Miss Arnold taught them how to do it. This way they saw what each house was going to look like. This was the birth of Tompkinsville, Canada's first community of cooperative housing.

5

Mary Willa Littler
The Strangers' Grave

IN SPRINGHILL IN 1891, there was a coal mine explosion that took 125 lives. Most of the dead were buried there. Some were sent back home for burial, to places like Pictou, and Glace Bay and Iona in Cape Breton. Those who could not be identified were buried in a single grave in Springhill — known as "The Strangers' Grave."

Since 1981, by a process of elimination, Mary Willa Littler has been working to name the people in "The Strangers' Grave." Further, she has been placing granite markers at the graves she has found outside of Springhill, to let people passing by in Pictou or Glace Bay or Iona know that, buried here, is a person — a man or a boy — who died in the 1891 Explosion at Springhill.

Magnificent Obsessions

We talked with Mary Willa Littler in September 1996. We asked her, "Is this your first time in Glace Bay?"

MARY WILLA LITTLER: Actually, I haven't been here for about six years, for any length of time, for a few days at a time. But I came in July, and I made a little bit of headway, just on a short weekend. Of course, after I left, then Wally Buchanan, who's the caretaker up here at Greenwood Cemetery—he called Mrs. Clark after I left and said that he found what I was looking for.

I'd been looking for William Burchell for 15 years. I knew he was buried somewhere in the Glace Bay area. I knew he was from Caledonia Mines, according to the newspaper articles that I had from 1891.

And so I came to Cape Breton probably in the fall in 1986, the fall of '87, '88, '89. In 1990, I went as far as Iona. And I didn't come all the way to Glace Bay because time didn't permit and I wanted to place that marker at John Gillis's grave at that time, and I just thought—it's too much, to do a few things at the same time. So I went back home from Iona.

And then, it wasn't till last summer I came here to Glace Bay, just for the day, with my niece. And I brought some of these markers that I've been telling you about. [The markers are heavy granite stones, about 8 inches square, engraved with a pit helmet and the date, 1891.] And I left them here at Art Littler's house in Glace Bay. He and I are not related, but we're pretty good friends. So I left them at his house. And I said, I'll come back next year and do this, a little bit more research.

So I came in July. When I was here I thought, I'll call a funeral home and ask who the caretaker is of this Greenwood Cemetery, because I'd never been here before. I'd been to some other cemeteries in Glace Bay, and really done a lot of legwork. Instead of looking in books or making phone calls, I was actually *looking.* And so I spoke with Mr. Buchanan and he said, "My mother's from Springhill. My mother was born in Springhill." You know, like you can't get away from Springhill, can you?

Mary Willa at the grave of William Burchell

So, he took all the details and then he said he would get back to me. Anyway, I had just left Clark's house — well, I left Sunday, and on Tuesday he called them and said he found what I was looking for. The grave of William Burchell.

What a feeling! Like this morning, when we were over here before lunch. I said, Well, 15 years I've been looking for this grave. Now I'm kneeling on top of him! You know, I was looking at the headstone and trying to make sure that I was seeing everything that was there. It's clear, but I mean, you know, just — wow! what a feeling!

The first mayor of Glace Bay was David M. Burchell. And this is David M. Burchell's grave right here. And here is William Burchell right behind him. And they are brothers. I've established that now. They're both the sons of Peter Burchell and Ellen — and there are Peter and Ellen's graves next to William's. "Killed at the Springhill Colliery Explosion, February 21, 1891, age 22 years...."

(*Is there anyone else in the Greenwood Cemetery killed at Springhill, besides William Burchell?*) Possibly there may be, but there don't seem to be any records of his burial in this cemetery. His name is John Boyd. And he would have been Presbyterian by faith, as well as William Burchell, which kind of led me to this grave. Because some of the other ones, being Anglican or Roman Catholic, would have been in maybe some of the other cemeteries around this area. In particular I wasn't looking for anybody who was Anglican. But the fact that William Burchell and John Boyd would have been that same faith, it's possible that he might have been buried here as well. But there doesn't seem to be any indication of it yet.

I haven't given up. I'm going to the Hardwood Hill Cemetery in Sydney tomorrow morning and see if there's something there. There's a John Boyd living here in Glace Bay that I'm in touch with today, who's one of the descendants from another line of the same family, kind of. And he has some idea that John Boyd, killed in Springhill, is buried there in Hardwood Hill. So, we're going to follow that up tomorrow. And I haven't met John Boyd yet, so it's going to be kind of fun. 'Cause we've been speaking with each other over the years, but we've never met face-to-face yet!

I started in 1981 on a Canada Community Development Project. It was a federally funded project for the town of Springhill. And it was only six months of work. But I think I just got personally attached to it, and I don't know how to let go! And I'm not going to be able to let go until I feel that it is complete. Maybe they thought it was complete at the end of six months. But as far as I'm concerned—I mean, it's led me in all kinds of directions for the past 15 years, and led me to different areas to look for these graves.

(*What was the goal for the six-month project?*) Just to identify the graves in Springhill, and to mark them off. Like kind of identify where they were, who they were. Clean their graves, if there were any bushes or anything like that. And if something was like tipped a little ways, to make it stand up straight again, or anything like that. But that's all it was. (*"The graves in Springhill." Of who? Of any explosion, or just...?*) Just 1891. Because there were 125 killed in that explosion, men and boys.

But in the course of the research, I came across a reference to "The Strangers' Grave." And I was kind of intrigued by "The Strangers' Grave." (*What does that mean?*) Well, it means that there were men and boys who were strangers to the town of Springhill, without any friends or relatives to claim their bodies. So they're buried in this common lot in Springhill called "The Strangers' Grave" or "The Strangers' Lot."

And it didn't have any marker on it at all. If you were walking in the cemetery, you would not have known where it was at all. And my quest, I guess, at that time was to discover—where is it? It exists, where is it? So then the undertaker at the funeral home in Springhill—his name is Winfield Brown—he found a reference to it in his ledgers. And all it said was that the Strangers' Lot was located in Lot #74 in the south section. And it said, several buried in it, at the 1891 explosion. But "several" didn't answer—like, what does several mean? Like, what number do you put on several?

So anyway, I started looking through all kinds of newspapers. Of course, I already had lots of newspapers from 1891. You know, I was well into my research with the whole thing. But I started looking at newspapers, and it was saying that these strangers were buried in one lot, 16 feet by 16 feet, and it had been dug to a depth of 5 feet or 6 feet. And that all bodies were laid side by side. But it still wasn't saying how many. In one newspaper article, it actually said "10 or 12" would be buried there. Another statement that was made in another newspaper said it "would not exceed a dozen." But in the meantime I've spoken with the fellow who's been the gravedigger in Springhill for quite a number of years. And I asked him, just lately even, how many would be buried in a lot 16 by 16 feet. And he said no more than 8. And that's been my feeling for a long time, too, that there are probably 8. But now it's to find out who those 8 were.

But that kind of goes in another direction too. Because there were 21 taken away by rail. But it didn't say who those 21 were. Which makes it more complicated. So, I want to find out who those 21 were that were taken away by rail, and who were the ones that were the strangers. And maybe then I'll feel like it's coming together and it's complete.

Of the 21, I think maybe I have located about 18 that were

taken away by rail. I'm getting closer now, but it's been 15 years.

(*And how many are buried right at Springhill?*) There were 75 graves that we located and identified because they had markers similar to this. (*Markers that said something like, "Killed at Springhill."*) And it did say their name, yes. And then there are a couple of lots that don't have markers on them. But I'm certain because of the cemetery records.

(*Once you name those who are at Springhill and those who were taken away, then you feel you'll be able to name the people that are in "The Strangers' Grave."*) That's right. And although I guess they'll always be strangers, at least their names will hopefully be inscribed on the marker that is now there. There is a marker there now. There wasn't one in 1981 when I started the project. But now there is one.

(*Where else have you found graves?*) Pictou County. Stellarton, Westville. I've gone to Tatamagouche. There was one in Scoudouc, New Brunswick. Quite a few places, really. In Iona. In Port Hood.

(*And when you find these graves, what do you then do?*) Well then, I ask permission, and I place a small marker on the grave. And so far I have never been refused. *Mary Willa laughs.* But it just denotes that the fellow — whether he was a boy or whether he was a man — that he was a victim of that explosion. The marker has a small miner's hat on it, and the date 1891. It doesn't say Springhill or anything like that, just the date 1891. I just make sure that I find a prominent spot on the grave, and place the marker where it can be seen if somebody comes along and suddenly notices that it's there, that hopefully they'll say, "Oh, okay!" And they'll read what it says on the stone as well.

I have come across one fellow — the guy who is buried in Tatamagouche — it says nothing about Springhill. It just says, "Died February 21, 1891." Doesn't say where, what happened, or anything. So that little marker, hopefully somewhere down the road, somebody will see that little miner's hat and 1891, and they'll connect what that means.

(*What did you think you'd be doing, for the last 15 years?*) Oh, you know–I would have liked to have been employed at something. But nevertheless, this has been really interesting for me. And if I didn't have it, and being unemployed—it has provided me with some satisfaction and things like that, over these years of not being employed. I could be ready to go to work in a minute. But it's just the situation. You know, where things are right now. It's not getting any better, either. I'm certainly capable of working.... Then of course there are young people coming up, younger than me—what are they going to go through? What is going to happen with them?

(*AS I UNDERSTAND IT, you don't just find the grave, place the marker, and walk away.*) Actually, I like to try to contact somebody to get permission to do it, for one thing. Someone in authority that won't say, "Well, she just went along and did this, and didn't even ask permission!" So, it's just a formality, to do it. Family. Or whoever is in charge of the cemetery.

But sometimes I try to ask the family. If the family want to be there, that's great. Like, I placed a marker in Stellarton in 1992. And there was an older fellow, his name is Danny Hood—he's since passed away. But I think Danny was 82 when I went to place a marker on James Conway's grave. And a lady from Springhill who was 91 at that time. And it turns out that they were like maybe second or third cousins, but had no knowledge of each other until I put them together. She lived in Springhill and he lived in New Glasgow, and they had no idea of each other's existence until James Conway's grave was located, and they learned that I wanted to put a marker there.

So that's nice, to meet up with these people. To meet who they are, and sit. Hey, these are part of James Conway's family. You know, a hundred years later, it's interesting to see some of these people.

(*Now, are any Cape Bretoners buried at Springhill?*) Yes. There are quite a few. And probably the reason is because the family actually moved into Springhill and made it their home.

For example, Rory MacNeil was living in Springhill. And it appeared that his parents were in Iona, but his body didn't come back to Iona. There's a headstone in the cemetery in Springhill with his name on it. But I don't know the reason why. There had to be some circumstances that his body didn't return to Cape Breton. I've never figured that out.

I DOCUMENT INFORMATION about all fatalities in Springhill. Single mishaps as well as the 1891 explosion. I haven't touched the Springhill mine disasters of 1956 or '58 in too much detail.

(*By single mishap you mean....*) Single mishaps in the everyday workings. (*"Fall of the roof." "Number 1 slope which was on fire."*)

I actually raised money in Springhill to erect monuments in memory of all of these single mishaps. It took me two years from the time that I said I was going to do it until the monuments were in place, with 202 names on the monuments, of single mishaps. From April 15 of 1876 until April 15, 1969. The first fatality was April 15 and the last one was April 15. In Springhill. (*And there will be no more.*) No. The coal mines are closed in Springhill. So in a two-year time period, I accomplished a goal that some people said was impossible to do. I wanted it done, and I knew it could be done.

(*Have you found other Cape Bretoners from 1891?*) Thomas Rogers in Dominion. But I didn't have a marker with me to place—I didn't expect to find it. I wasn't looking for him being buried in Dominion. It was a surprise to me. I'm hoping to go there Monday afternoon and place a marker there.

(*And the one at Iona....*) That's John Gillis. (*Have you placed a marker there yet?*) Actually, here's the marker I placed on his grave. *Mary Willa showed a photo of a full-sized gravestone rather than the little marker.* That's not what I normally place. Because it was quite important to me. This one was different. (*John Gillis—why was that different?*) Because of this letter I received from Mr. Neil J. Gillis. Here is the original letter I sent to him in December of 1981:

Dear Mr. Gillis, I am writing in reference to the Springhill Explosion, the 21st of February, 1891. A Canada Community Development Project under the title of Community Restoration has undertaken the work of locating the areas designated for the burial of these explosion victims. To date we have located 80 graves of the 125 victims. My query is: one of the victims was a single man, 24 years of age, from Jamesville, Victoria County, Cape Breton, named John Gillis. I'm wondering if it is possible that his remains were brought back to that area, and perhaps buried in a family lot. And, he may have been a relative to you. Any assistance you can give me in this matter will be greatly appreciated. Sincerely yours, Mary Willa Littler, Project Manager, Community Restoration Project.

And here is his answer to me. He just turned the page over and answered on the back of the same letter. Neil John Gillis wrote:

The John Gillis who was killed in the Springhill Explosion, 1891, was my uncle. I heard my father say that he was 17 years old when he was killed. His body was being claimed by another family, until he was positively identified by one other man from Iona. He, Alex P. MacNeil, knew that one-half of one of John Gillis's ears was bitten

John Gillis and his gravestone

off by a horse when he was very small. Sincerely, Neil Gillis. [And, he also wrote:] John Gillis buried in the parish cemetery, Iona, Nova Scotia, south of the church. No grave marker. N.J.G. Neil John Gillis.

And, of course, when I saw that statement, "no grave marker," I thought, if there was some way that I could do it, that eventually I would make sure that there was a marker put there. I wrote back to Mr. Gillis right away, but I never heard from him any more. And then in 1989 I came up to Cape Breton. The train was still running to Cape Breton then. I got off that train at Iona and I stayed at the Highland Heights Inn. And I called Mr. Gillis and asked him if he would take me to the cemetery and show me where John Gillis's grave was located. And after I went home again, I made arrangements to have the marker made at Tingley's Monument Works in Amherst. And they made a lovely marker.

And the next year I got in touch with Mr. and Mrs. Gillis to make sure that they would be home, because I wanted to bring this marker to them. They wanted me staying at their house, and things like this. And so I stayed with them, and met some other members of the family, and saw where John Gillis was brought up on the property that he lived in when he was a youngster.

THIS LETTER IS FROM ANOTHER FELLOW in Mabou — John Gillies, a schoolteacher. And he says that he had heard that I was looking for information about Joshua MacNeil, who was killed in Springhill. He says:

Joshua MacNeil was a native of Port Hood. His name appears in the 1871 Canadian census. And he is listed as a 4-year-old boy, indicating that he was born in 1867, the year of Canadian confederation. His father was John MacNeil, born in Nova Scotia, and his mother was the first wife of John MacNeil, Elizabeth Ellen Bull, who was born in Prince Edward Island. Joshua MacNeil was born and raised on a small mixed farm owned by his parents on the Irish Road in the district of Port Hood. His ethnic origin was Irish and his religion was Presbyterian. Joshua's father John was the son of William and Catherine, who were both born in Ireland. Joshua had brothers David, John Robert, and Charlie, and sisters Jane, Sarah, and Christena.

Joshua MacNeil still has a stepbrother living in the Glencoe Station area of Port Hood district. He came as an English orphan to the MacNeil farm on May 24, 1920, when John MacNeil was 80 years of age. John MacNeil died in 1928. (Joshua's) stepbrother's name is John Guest. John Guest has told me that he often heard his stepfather speak about Joshua. Joshua apparently was a favourite son, and the father never fully recovered from the mining death of his son. He had a picture of his son Joshua always on display in the house.

The fact that Joshua followed mining was not unusual in that mining was one of the main pillars of Port Hood's economy in the late 1800s and early 1900s. Many miners came out of the Port Hood districts....

So, I have proof that Joshua MacNeil was brought to Port Hood, but there's no physical evidence at his father's grave. I went to Port Hood and visited with John Guest, with John Gillies. John Guest was full of information, and just a really interesting fellow. But when we went to the cemetery, we found Joshua's father's headstone, and the fact that it said that John MacNeil died in 1928. But we couldn't see anything for Joshua. John Guest was always calling him "Joshuway." And I really enjoyed that—Joshuway.

(*So did you put a marker in that area?*) I didn't because I couldn't physically find something. And if ever I can establish that it's to the left or to the right of his father's grave, you know—I'm going to do something some day.

(*You set a nice example.*) Thank you. (*You don't boast or brag about this, you just do this. Why?*) Oh, I don't know how to let go of it. *Mary Willa chuckles.* I don't know why.

Mary Willa found Thomas Rogers' grave. His stone is located in Dominion, Cape Breton, across from the I.O.C. Hall. He was 21 when he died in 1891, and was survived by his mother. He was a native of Old Bridgeport, Cape Breton—the sole support of his mother. He and his mother had come to Springhill after the explosion in the Ford Pit in 1880, when his father was a victim of that disaster, along with 41 others.

Another one of the victims of the 1891 Explosion at Springhill was Thomas Davis, age 14. He was the son of Thomas and Annie Davis and the older brother of William Davis, who later went to New Waterford, Cape Breton. At the age of 37 William Davis was shot during the miners' strike, June 11, 1925—a murder commemorated by the annual Miners' Memorial Day.

Mary Willa found the grave of Hugh M. Robinson. At 31, he left behind a wife and three children. He was a native of Lancashire, England. His remains were numbered as the 104th body taken out of the mine at Springhill on Monday, February 23, 1891. After the explosion, Mrs. Robinson and her children re-located to Port Morien, Cape Breton, where some of the descendants of Hugh M. Robinson reside today. The grave of Hugh M. Robinson is located in Hillside Cemetery, south section, Springhill.

1891 Springhill Explosion Victims with a Cape Breton Connection

The asterisk (*) indicates graves located in Hillside Cemetery, Springhill, N.S.

The plus sign (+) indicates graves located in other places.

+**BOYD, John** 21 b. Mira, s/o Norman & Mary Boyd. Buried in Hardwood Hill Cemetery, Sydney. +**BURCHELL, William** 22 son of Peter & Ellen Burchell. Buried in Greenwood Cemetery, Glace Bay *CAMPBELL, Donald** 47 native of Bridgend, Cape Breton. **CAMPBELL, John D.** 24 nephew of Donald, from Cape Breton, locality not yet known, grave not yet located. *FINLAYSON, Daniel** 29 from the Middle River area of Victoria Co., Cape Breton. **+GILLIS, John** 17 from Jamesville, Victoria Co., Cape Breton. Buried in Iona, Cape Breton. **LIVINGSTON, Henry** 24 b. 30 March 1867, baptized 9 April 1867, Low Point, Cape Breton. **MURPHY Richard** 21 from Sydney Mines. **McDONALD, John J.** 42 from Cape Breton, locality not yet known. Grave not yet located. ***McDONALD, Rory B.** 40 reported to be from Cape Breton, locality not yet known. **MacKINNON. Angus** 51 born at Long Island, Cape Breton. ***McLEOD, Neil J.** 23 reported to be from Cape Breton, locality not yet known. ***McLEOD, Rory (Roderick)** 29 born at Big Intervale, Cape Breton. **McNEIL, John F.** 32 reported to be from Glace Bay, Cape Breton. **MacNEIL, Joshua** 21 from Port Hood, Cape Breton. Remains forwarded there, grave not yet located. **McNEIL, Neil S.** 23 died one week after, remains brought to Cape Breton, possibly Glace Bay. ***MacNEIL, Roderick D.** 25 from Iona, Victoria Co., Cape Breton. ***McPHEE, Neil** 28 from Reserve Mines, Cape Breton. **NEARING, James** 20 b. 27 February 1870, Lingan, Cape Breton. Son of John Nearing (info below). **NEARING, John** 50 born in North Sydney, Cape Breton. Father of James and Malcolm. **NEARING, Malcolm** 22 b. 27 June 1868, Glace Bay, Cape Breton. Son of John Nearing (info above). ***NICHOLSON, Malcolm** 42 born in Cape Breton, locality not yet known. **+ROGERS, Thomas** 21 native of Old Bridgeport, Cape Breton. Buried in Dominion, Cape Breton.

6

A Talk on the Rocks!
Cape Breton's Geology

Robert Raeside

C APE BRETON HAS NOT ALWAYS been surrounded by water. Cape Breton has not always ridden on the surface of the earth, and it has not always been in the northern hemisphere. The story of its moves and transformations can be read through its geol-ogy—the rocks we find today. And in terms of geology, Cape Breton Island was only discov-ered in the 1980s!

DR. ROB RAESIDE: Cape Breton Island is really the—well, it was the centre of the world, back three or four hundred mil-lion years ago! It was right in the middle of a huge continent which stretched from California to China. And it was probably buried 30 kilometres down in the crust of the earth, at the

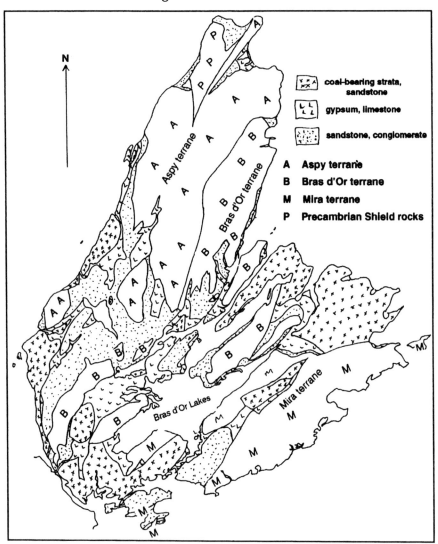

A simple map of Cape Breton showing the four zones (Canadian Shield, Aspy terrane, Bras d'Or terrane, and Mira terrane) and the overlying sedimentary rocks (gypsum and limestone, sandstone, and coal-bearing units). See text on page 53.

middle of where a large ocean basin had recently closed up, within the previous 20 million years. And as a result of that, its geological history is very, very complex.

When we first mapped the geology—the bedrocks of Cape Breton in 1983, '84, '85—we were encountering one new rock type every day. And I suspect that there is probably a greater variety of igneous rocks—plutonic rocks that were once magmas—in the Cape Breton Highlands than there is anywhere else, certainly in North America and perhaps anywhere in the world except along the Himalayas or the Alps.

But that's all been eroded down through the last three hundred million years. We talk of that as the recent past—three hundred million years or so. And now it's exposed for a view. We were so excited when we first mapped that area. It had never really been looked at by geologists before. We didn't know what we were going to find when we went in there. And it was really thrilling. It was a sense of discovery. It was like what the explorers must have felt when they first found places like North America. We were finding these rocks for the first time. Every bend in the river was something new.

Unfortunately, that's gone. We've now been up every brook in Cape Breton Highlands and we've been down all the rivers and all the logging roads. So we're not going to find anything new. But we're still doing detailed scientific measurements and work and—more lab work, now, rather than field work.

But the initial sense of discovery of this centre of tectonic activity—which is the mountain-building activity that forced Africa into North America and sent up this huge mountain range—that was the initial discovery. And it's such a narrow little belt here in Cape Breton. It expands to be something the width of the whole of the island of Newfoundland or the whole of the Appalachians when you get down into America. But here in Cape Breton it's all squeezed into just 150 kilometres.

So, we've got an exciting story. We're really at a fulcrum of the Appalachian origin, a centre of the Devonian world. And we've enjoyed working that story out. We've enjoyed trying to figure out what all the little pieces are that were players in it.

In the far north we've got the Pre-Cambrian Shield. Down in southern Nova Scotia, we've got a fragment of Africa. That's south of a line from Canso to Truro. And everything between that line and the Cape North region is what was scattered out across an ocean. And was eventually all squeezed together and compressed to make a mountain range that was the height of the Himalayas

300-odd million years ago, and has now been worn down.

In a nutshell, that's the story. All the details account for all the debris and bits and pieces of islands, and continental plateaus, and things that sit out in oceans. And they all got scraped off and plastered against North America when Africa bumped into it, 360 million years ago. And that's the story that we're trying to unravel in detail now.

In the last couple of million years or so, we have the Ice Age. We sometimes say the ice sheets surged across, but they only moved centimetres a year. But they came across the continent. They came out across Cape Breton and Nova Scotia, far off onto the Continental Shelf. Then they melted back. And this happened four or six or twenty times, depending on who you listen to. And the ice sheets scraped off the surface material and exposed the bedrock, and filled up the valleys with all kinds of boulders and sand, and the deposits which are now quarried for road metal and so on, around Middle River and such like. And left the Highlands available for us to see.

And included with that, there's a really interesting climatic history. Because, it got cold, but then it got warmer than it is now. The climate has fluctuated between something which is more akin to Greenland and something which is more akin to Georgia—oh, four or five times over the last million years. And we're somewhere in between at the moment, in the climate that we have today. That climate history is documented from the deposits in some of the lakes—the Bras d'Or Lake in particular, which is very deep and has got deep mud deposits in it.

So that's a different part of the history, and that might be a different story.

In a nutshell, that's what's happened to Cape Breton to make it the way it is. It's part of a much larger mountain chain that stretches from Alabama right up through Nova Scotia into Newfoundland. And then across the Atlantic through France and Britain into Norway. And even further north along the east coast of Greenland. The Atlantic Ocean is a young thing which opened up—split the giant continent apart, and left Nova Scotia on the west side and took Britain over to the east side. But geologically, they're very similar to each other. They're part and parcel of the same mountain belt.

The red sandstones that you see here in Nova Scotia are the same red sandstones that were called the "Old Red Sandstones" by the first geologists 200 years ago in Britain. They are the same age, with the same fossils. And in some cases almost the same sequence of rocks: sandstone, covered by limestone, covered by gypsum. And we see that over in Britain as well.

I don't know how much more I can say without going into details!

I can tell you what the framework, the basic skeleton of Cape Breton Island is made up from. We have surveyed all the Highlands. We haven't actually worked on many of the Lowlands. But the Highlands are the things that tell the old story. The Lowlands tell a more recent story, and then the Ice Age, the most recent story of all.

The Highland areas have got the most complex and the longest geological history.

We have to go back about 1400 million years or so, to get the very beginning of it. And that's right up in northernmost Cape Breton Island. Bordered by Pollet's Cove on the west, and a rather difficult-to-find line which runs from Cape North right down along the North Mountain. Not the Aspy Fault itself, but another fault which is a little bit inland. Five kilometres inland from the Aspy Fault there's another line which marks these very old rocks.

These rocks had been known about for many, many years, and no one really knew what they were. One of the main rock types that's in there is called anorthosite. Anorthosite is a rock that formed in the earth about 1500 to 1100 million years ago. It's a magmatic rock—that is, it was a rock which formed by melting deep down in the crust of the earth, and ponding as great reservoirs of magma, and gradually crystallizing to form solid rock. And there are many of these anorthosites scattered across the Pre-Cambrian Shields of the world. There are huge areas up in Quebec and Labrador, and also in Australia and in Africa. In the old continental cores.

Nova Scotia's supposed to be relatively young, geologically.

Why do we have these old rocks up in there? Eventually we twigged to the thought that maybe this is part of the Pre-Cambrian Shield that's been caught up or preserved in northern Cape Breton. And when we analysed the isotopes of the elements in the rock, we discovered that, lo and behold, it was very old. It gave an age of over a billion years.

So that rock is, indeed, part of the Pre-Cambrian Shield. Whether or not it's still connected to the Pre-Cambrian Shield, we don't know. Maybe it's been jostled around a little bit. But there are rocks that are very similar, near Stephenville in Newfoundland, and all the way up the Great Northern Peninsula of Newfoundland. So that we feel fairly confident that we're dealing with something which was the edge of the ancient Pre-Cambrian continent of North America. Before Africa and South America arrived and bumped into North America.

If you go to the other side of Cape Breton altogether, we have an area which we call the Mira terrane. It stretches from Scatarie Island, right down through towards Sporting Mountain near West Bay. And everything south and east of a line which is the MacIntosh Brook Fault. It lies just east of the Boisdale Hills. Everything south and east of that line is about 600 million years old. And these rocks are pretty near identical, unit for unit, with rocks in the Avalon Peninsula of Newfoundland. And they also extend out through the Antigonish Highlands and the Cobequid Highlands to New Brunswick, and even down into New England.

Similar rocks occur in old England, and Wales, and over in France, and out through Germany into Czechoslovakia.

This looks like it was something else — on the other side of an ancient ocean. These rocks are rocks that were formed in a volcanic arc — somewhat like Japan today, perhaps. Something that would be sitting off the edge of a continent, where a piece of the ocean floor is diving down underneath the continent's edge. And as it dives down it melts, and lava rises up to the surface and makes volcanoes. And we have many volcanic rocks.

And in fact, at Louisbourg Harbour is one of the best places to see these volcanic rocks. You can see volcanic bombs, where great boulders of material erupted from volcanoes and landed in the muds and the sands around. You can even see the plop marks where they landed. You see volcanic glass—pumice, and all kinds of relics of volcanic material, exposed quite well in the Fortress of Louisbourg National Historic Park, and especially well across the harbour, from where you can look across to the park.

So that sort of sets a framework. These are the old parts of Cape Breton. Between them we have two more slivers of rock. We have the Bras d'Or terrane, which basically lies within and around the Bras d'Or Lakes, and extends up the eastern Cape Breton Highlands to Ingonish. And then we have the Aspy terrane, which is the youngest of them. And that extends from Cape North and Ingonish on the east, down through to Chéticamp and Mabou on the west. [See the Terrane Map on page 48.]

First of all, the older ones—they're about 550 million years old. This is the Bras d'Or terrane. This was another island arc, a bit younger than the Mira terrane that we talked about earlier. The Bras d'Or terrane is made up of the rocks that we find today in a subduction zone. This is a zone where one piece of the ocean floor is diving down underneath another piece of ocean floor. That's happening today, for example, around the islands of the Caribbean. Or some of the small island arcs like the Philippines, or the Marianas Islands in the west Pacific.

And as one piece of ocean crust is pushed down underneath another piece of ocean crust, it melts. And volcanoes arise at the surface. And lots of magma gets ponded at great depth. And in fact if you travel from the junction of the Cabot Trail and Highway 312 at Jersey Cove or Barachois River, along the Cabot Trail and (inland) up the Wreck Cove Road towards the west, you're actually driving down the subduction zone—the ancient 550-million-year-old subduction zone. The rocks at the junction of 312 and the Cabot Trail are volcanic rocks. They must have been erupted on the sea floor.

Then you encounter a type of granite—they call it granodiorite—of the Indian Brook plutonic mass. And that granodiorite was intruded into the crust, but just below the volcanic rocks. You can actually see the contact exposed at that road junction.

Then as you go up onto the hills, you are actually going

deeper down into the crust. The whole thing has been tipped up on end. And by the time we get across to the western edge of all those plutonic magmatic masses—you're down to somewhere like 30 kilometres down in the crust. And then you encounter some rocks which were once beach deposits, but have been dragged down into the crust.

(*You keep saying "down," but actually you've travelled up onto the Highlands—is that because it was down?*) It *was* down. And now everything has been brought back up to the surface. It's bounced back up after the subduction process stopped, after the ocean floor stopped going down underneath. And the rocks along the coast perhaps bounced up five kilometres. But the rocks in the middle have bounced up 30 kilometres. They've rebounded that much further. Because they had been dragged down a lot further.

(*So although we're travelling up into the Highlands, we're going down....*) Down into the crust. We're going down to great depths—30 kilometres, 20 miles down beneath the surface of the earth. And the rocks that we see exposed there [at the surface, in the centre of the Highlands] today are the kinds of rocks that are now forming 20 or 30 kilometres underneath the Philippine Islands or the Caribbean Islands today.

Now, if you go a little bit further, suddenly everything changes. A major fault zone runs from the Ingonish area, down through the central Highlands to Baddeck. And it continues underneath younger rocks which have buried it, out towards the west. It's coming out to shore near Port Hood. This line is a major fault zone. Two blocks of rock were grinding past each other for many millions of years, and have totally shattered and pulverized the rock into a very, very fine-grained rock mass. Which is totally unrecognizable today—you would never know what the original rock used to be.

We've mapped this trail of destruction up here from the middle of the Cape Breton Highlands right on towards Ingonish. Unfortunately—or perhaps interestingly—there's a younger rock which has intruded into it, and it doesn't ever really come to the shore very well. But you can certainly see it in some of the logging roads in the centre of Cape Breton Highlands.

And that marks the boundary between the Bras d'Or terrane and some of this youngest terrane—the Aspy terrane. We've moved into the ages of rocks when fossils are preserved in them. Though these rocks have all been baked and stewed so much that the fossils are all now unrecognizable. Their ages are around about 430 to 370 million years old. And they include some very complex schists and gneisses, in the headwaters of the Aspy Rivers in particular. And also in the Jumping Brook area.

And later on, these were intruded by granites. The Margaree granite on the west side, and the Black Brook granite coming out at Neil's Harbour on the east side, are two examples of that.

But what was happening here was that we had another sliver of rocks caught between the vices of two continents moving along. You remember I said earlier that the ocean plates were moving down a subduction zone. But those ocean plates also carried on them, like a piggyback rider, fragments of continent. One of these continental fragments by this time was probably South America. It's preserved today—a remnant of South America is preserved as the Mira terrane of southeastern Cape Breton. Another was North America, carried on a different plate. And its remnant is the northwestern Highlands, by Pollett's Cove.

As those two continental fragments approached each other, the continental rocks are lighter than the ocean-floor rocks, and they can't go down the subduction zone. They're too buoyant. They won't sink down into the mantle of the earth. So what happens is that all the ocean floor gets pushed down, or sucked down, the subduction zone. And these two large fragments of continents come together. And it's just like two cars meeting head on—at the speed of 10 centimetres a year! And they collide. But the forces are so immense and so powerful that the collision perhaps goes on for 20 million years before everything finally comes to a grinding halt. And by the time this has happened, a huge mountain range has been forced up.

We know from the kinds of minerals that are preserved in the central Cape Breton Highlands, west of Chéticamp Lake, that that area was covered by mountains which were at least 30 kilometres above where we are today. Now, no mountain ever gets to be 30 kilometres high because the rain and the snows will wear it away very fast. But we're looking at a mountain range which was probably at least as high as the Himalayas are today, centred on central Cape Breton Highlands. And extending all the way down the Appalachians towards Alabama, and across Newfoundland and into Britain and Norway on the other side.

(*All connected?*) All connected. There was no Atlantic Ocean at the time. It was all part of one mountain belt. When you start getting such a deep mountain belt, it gets very hot down there. The rocks begin to melt, and granite is produced. Granite is the melted component of the roots of that mountain chain. And these plutons—those granite masses at Neil's Harbour and Margaree, and some more scattered—and all the granites down in southern Nova Scotia—were all produced at the same time, when this material was all crumpled together and a great mountain mass was pushed up.

Well there's the framework of the story. We have the four different blocks. The old, billion-year and more, Pre-Cambrian Shield in the north. We have the 600-million-year-old volcanic arc which became a continental fragment, in the south, along the Mira terrane. Then we have another subduction zone arc like the Philippines, which became the Bras d'Or terrane. And then at the very end, a continental collision when the two continental fragments arrived and smashed into each other and dragged the Aspy terrane down into the crust, from which it has since rebounded. That melted at that time and produced all the granites that we see scattered throughout the Aspy terrane.

By this time Cape Breton Island, or the Appalachian system as a whole, was really at the centre of a huge continent which stretched all the way from California on the west side of North America right across—without any ocean interruption—as far as Siberia or China or East Africa. Cape Breton was far from the sea. We were in the southern latitudes, somewhere around the Tropic of Capricorn. And the climate was hot, the climate was dry. And the mountains began to wear away. And great desert sandstones and gravel deposits were quickly laid down. Those are very visible today. They're referred to as the Horton Group, because they were first identified at Horton, near Wolfville. But they are exposed particularly around the Trans-Canada Highway at Salt Mountain near Whycocomagh.

But these red sandstones are found throughout Cape Breton and mainland Nova Scotia. And these were the sandstones that were the sands and gravels that were being washed off the mountains, and were being deposited in the valleys and the basins that formed after the mountains were heaved up.

I MENTIONED THAT THE TWO CONTINENTS had collided. What collided was probably South America with North America. The west coast of South America had collided with the east coast of North America. But the forces that had caused that collision were still in operation. There were some remnant forces still going on. And gradually, South America was pushed sideways, towards the left, North America towards the right. And Africa moved in in place of it. Africa and South America were joined together; there was no Atlantic Ocean between them at that time.

So you can imagine this great sideways motion of North America moving northwards to the right, South America moving southwards to the left, out of the way, and Africa moving in in place of it.

All that area of Nova Scotia which lies south of a line from Canso to Truro—that's a portion of Africa. We refer to it as the Meguma terrane. The rocks that we see in Nova Scotia today are like rocks in Morocco.

(*So we're not simply saying that it's the same rock that you would find there. We're saying, it is a portion of Africa that has remained here when the rest of Africa split away.*) That's right. (*And we're not saying that these are like the rocks of South America, here along the Mira coast or Framboise or Louisbourg. We're not saying it's very similar. We're saying, it is the same thing as a portion of South America that tore away when South America itself went into place.*) That's what we're saying.

These rocks in the Louisbourg area actually were formed on the west coast of ancient South America. When South America slid out sideways out of the way, these rocks were left behind, as a souvenir of South America's visit to Cape Breton!

(*And once again, here in the north we're looking at the formation of the Pre-Cambrian Shield.*) Which is part of North America, and is very similar to Pre-Cambrian Shield rocks still exposed in Labrador and Quebec and Ontario today.

So we have these large forces with continents moving sideways. And when continents move sideways, inevitably there are going to be little irregularities: bits that stick out into the ocean or bits that stick out into the other continent. It's not a clean cut—it's a very ragged tear. And as a result, there are lots of little basins that open up—little holes that seem to open up in the continental crust. And these were the basins that very quickly filled up with the sediment that was being eroded off the mountaintops.

Sandstone. Limestones and gypsum of the Windsor group. These were sediments. (*As those Himalayan mountains wore down.*) Yes. As they wore down, and as any holes opened up in them, we had sediment being deposited. Every time you get a bowl-shaped depression in the surface of the earth, it fills up with sediment.

At first it was the sandstone, because the mountains were very high. Then we moved into a period when Cape Breton had moved a little bit further north into equatorial latitudes—somewhere around about the latitude of Brazil or Zaire today. Hot, sticky, lots of precipitation. And much of the mountains had really been worn away by this time. This would perhaps be about 20 or 30 million years later. We're looking at a period about 350 million years ago. And a shallow arm of the sea flooded across much of North America. It extended probably in from both coasts—from the eastern Chinese coast and the western Californian coast. And this arm of the sea was periodically cut off from the main ocean. And as a result, the seawater would all evaporate away. And we were left with big deposits of gypsum—the calcium sulfate formed.

And you see these deposits of gypsum well exposed on the Cabot Trail at Cape North. And you see them particularly well in the cliffs at Big Harbour. It's mined at Little Narrows. That gypsum was all deposited in a very shallow sea sitting on top of the continent; in a downright hot environment.

Eventually those seas filled up with more mud and more limestone and more sediment, and we ended up getting the coal measures of Cape Breton—of the Sydney and Glace Bay area—being laid down. These are laid down in limestones and sandstones. And they are the product of an equatorial forest—a rainforest like we see in Brazil or Zaire or Indonesia today. I don't know so much about the coal seams in Cape Breton, but I know that they're thick and they are certainly very abundant. And they're very similar to the coal seams in Britain, and in France and Germany. They're all the same age. They were deposited in the Carboniferous Period. We're talking about fairly recent history, compared to the older part of Cape Breton. We're talking about 300-or-so million years ago.

(*When you say deposit, what we really are saying is that this was a forest in another latitude*....) In an equatorial latitude, as Nova Scotia gradually moved northwards across the globe. (*This forest grew, fell, and became compressed.*) It rotted away, and the carbon organic material became compressed into seams of coal. And every now and again a river would flood across those probably ancient peat bogs and bury them with another layer of sandstone. So we have got a top to the coal seam. And then another forest would develop on top of that sand, and another coal seam would be developed.

So we've got a sequence of coal seam upon coal seam. Meaning: forest, drowned by sand; another forest developing on that, drowned by sand again; and so on, up through the maybe 20 or 30 million years of time.

And while this process is taking place, Cape Breton is gradually moving northwards at a speed somewhere from two to three centimetres a year. And that really is about the end of the story. Because from then until the Ice Age, there really isn't any record of what was happening in Cape Breton. Probably, Cape Breton was all above the waves at that time. It was not buried by any sea or ocean. It was a block of rock in the middle of a continent. If you think of somewhere like the centre of Asia—somewhere in

Mongolia just now—that would be the sort of environment that Cape Breton experienced through the next couple of hundred million years of time. We have no record of rocks in that time anywhere in the island, so we don't really know what was going on. We refer to that as our missing volumes.

(*In other words, everything that we've talked about here is the condition up to that period. Which is—do we date that period?*) The youngest rock that we have is referred to as the Pictou group. It's exposed on the shores of Bay St. Lawrence, and I believe is also exposed in some of the areas around by North Sydney to Point Aconi. And I'm not sure exactly of its age, but it's going to be on the order of, perhaps 300 million years or so. The Pictou group is the name of the youngest formation. And in Cape Breton Island, it's made of sandstones, siltstones, shales, coals, and conglomerates.

Basically, throughout that last 290 million years of time, Cape Breton has been dry land. And when a piece of land is above the ocean waves, it doesn't really collect sediment. Sediment is washed off it, and so there's no record, really, of what was happening. Nothing was being laid down to record the passage of time. And nothing was rising up. It was a stable continent—as stable as the heart of North America is today.

That's why there's no story. No magma is being produced, no volcanoes, no plutons. Any rocks that are being worn away, the material is simply being taken off by some great river and deposited far, far away.

(*So this is the stable period.*) This is the stable period. One of the things that had to happen during that stable period, of which we don't really have any record, is the formation of the Atlantic Ocean. Cape Breton is washed by the shores of the Atlantic today. But 350 million years ago, you could walk from Cape Breton to Britain, or from mainland Nova Scotia to Morocco. So somehow the Atlantic had to be formed. And that happened in the Jurassic Period, perhaps some 200 million years ago.

A great fracture must have opened up, quite far to the east of Cape Breton, off the edge of the continental shelf—out beyond Sable Island. And new ocean floor lavas rose up. And gradually

A Talk on the Rocks! Cape Breton's Geology

Cape Breton moved westwards at about 10 centimetres a year, relative to Britain and Africa, which was moving eastwards at the same time. You can think of it as a conveyor-belt system, whereby lava is being produced in the centre, and the two blocks are gradually separating themselves apart.

And when we go and we look at the rocks in the Atlantic Ocean today, sure enough, the rocks against Cape Breton are the same age as the rocks against Britain. And as you go towards the centre of the Atlantic Ocean they get younger and younger, until you reach the Azores in the middle, where they're less than a million years old. So we've got the whole record out there in the ocean floor lavas, but we don't see any remains of that on land, because this was all above the waves.

However, we do see offshore some sediment that was being washed off the new continent of North America, and was being deposited. And the oil exploration has really shown us lots of detail about the buildup of sedimentary rock, which records the separation of Africa and Europe from North America. But there's nothing on land that would ever lead you to suggest that there was going to be a great ocean basin opening up at that time. Everything is very quiet and very gentle — no great mountain-building event at all.

And that's still going on. Britain is still receding from North America at the rate of about 10 centimetres a year. They're still moving apart. There is a continual ocean-floor spreading process.

Throughout the time period — this period which we refer to as the "missing pages" of the geological history of Cape Breton — the climate was fairly warm. At first we were in the latitudes of the Sahara Desert. There are some sandstones down in the Annapolis Valley which record that time period. Then things got a little bit cooler. We moved into a climate perhaps more akin to that of the southern United States. And as Nova Scotia and North America in general moved northwards, we moved into a more northerly climate.

But the culmination of that came when the climate became very unstable about 2 million years ago. No one really knows why the climate started to become unstable. This is a bit of a puzzle. But we start to see big swings in average world temperature. It started to get very cold. And then it would warm up again quickly. When I say quickly, I'm referring to over a period of perhaps 50 or 100 thousand years. When it got cold, the rain would fall as snow, ice would build up on land. Glaciers would build up on any high land and moved southwards, crawling at very slow rates as far as about New York City.

Then it would melt back for a while, and the climate would warm. And in this period Cape Breton experienced alternating ice ages and warm periods. The climate would fluctuate from that of Greenland today to that of the Carolinas or Georgia. And at the moment we're probably in between two of these ice advances. We don't know when the next one will come, or if it ever will. But the chances are that if things go on the way they've been going on for the last 2 million years, in another 50 thousand years time, ice will again cover Cape Breton.

We've been able to record this movement of the glaciers moving back and forward because of the very deep waters of the Bras d'Or Lake, particularly the St. Andrews Channel, which goes down some 700 feet below sea level. In that area the ice never quite reached bottom. So sediment continued to gather in St. Andrews Channel. And drilling out there has brought back a record of mud and silt which contain the pollen grains of the plants that grew at the time. So you see Arctic species being replaced by a layer of hickory wood and bass wood that only grows in the southern States today, being replaced by northern pine forests, being replaced by beechwood forests, and so on. More southern beechwood forests than the ones typical of Cape Breton today.

And through this pollen record we've been able to chart the advance and retreat of the glaciers, up until the present period when we are in what's referred to as a northern boreal climate position. And we see the balsa fir and spruce forests in the up-lands, and the beech and little bit oak and maple forests in the lowlands today.

One of the advantages to a geologist of the Ice Age is that it has scraped everything clean — we can see the rocks. If I were to do this sort of work in the southern United States, I would have to take a shovel out and dig my rocks up. Because they're all covered; they're all weathered deeply, and they're all soft and converted to clays. But the ice has scraped all that off Cape Breton. And because of these ice ages we've been able to look at the bare bones—the framework—of the island, and we are able to recognize all the bedrock types.

When you get up on top of the Cape Breton Highlands sometimes in the summertime, you think the ice isn't all that far away either. And the wind is blowing across it. But it has been a great advantage for us to try to unravel the history of the island.

And that pretty well brings us up to the present day. The ice left deposits of soil—of sand and gravel—in many places. And that of course has been quarried for many years. Some of the large quarries in the Middle River valley in particular are very well exploited and have been used for the production of road metal and such like.

But that brings us up to the modern day, when we have a natural vegetation of northern boreal forests, which cover most of the island with more Arctic taiga and tundra conditions in the higher altitudes of the Cape Breton Highlands. Rocks are still being laid down in the form of sediment. And in fact, the area along the northern third of the island—around the Cape Breton Highlands—probably looks very similar today to what it must have looked like back in the Devonian time period. Except, of course, it's not a hot area today—it's very cold. But the high hills of the Cabot Trail are probably similar to the high mountains that must have been raised up by those Devonian mountain-building events 350 to 370 million years ago.

Probably the reason for our interest in Cape Breton has been the complexity in such a small area.

And much of this is very visible, if you take the time to look at the rocks, the outcrops around the Cabot Trail. Take the time to look at the outcrops anywhere you see rocks poking through the surface on our highways and on the byways. Yes indeed, you can see the effects of it. You can observe the red sandstones—very visible in many road cuts because they are lower lying areas, and that's where many people have lived, and settlement has occurred. Roads go through those areas.

But around the Cabot Trail, for example, you see the granites well exposed along the area from Ingonish to Neil's Harbour. You see the effects of the thrusting and pushing of portions of the mountain belt in the cliff at La Grande Falaise at Chéticamp. Or you can see the volcanic rocks at the Englishtown junction on the Cabot Trail. So those things are all very visible today. And basically anywhere where you see rock outcrops you are seeing some small part of that long billion-year past history that's made Cape Breton Island.

Dr. Rob Raeside and his team have already produced a remarkable "Geological Highway Map of Nova Scotia." That map is a map to *read*! It is available through the Nova Scotia Map Store, http://www.gov.ns.ca/snsmr/maps/.

Robert Raeside among boulders along the Clyburn River

7

Social Worker Visits Cape Breton, 1925

Sara M. Gold

T HIS ARTICLE BEGINS with a portrait of the growth of corporate industry in Cape Breton, and then sets that against a description of the lives of the workers in that industry—all in the context of the 1925 coal strike.

SARA M. GOLD: Because we today are born into a ready-made world we take its existence in the past for granted; and we accept the methods of acquiring, making and distributing the things in it, as deep-rooted, ever-present, unchangeable laws. We are too prone to simply accept, ungratefully use, and never question how our present life came to be.

It is not quite our

fault. We live in a mechanical civilization. Life is automatically easy. To our doorstep, at our finger-ends, to our bidding, come flying from all corners of the earth, all sorts of objects to minister to our every want, to our every idea of comfort and pleasure.... The method of making [these objects], the life and energy used up, is obscured. Too often, in the industrial circle do we see the important-looking and awe-inspiring owners of goods. We do not usually see the makers of goods, the workers. They are hidden by the array of costly machinery, buildings, fine offices, lawbooks, government machinery, regiments of police and soldiers. And so everything that is, becomes sanction for what was and will be. We are lulled into a belief that society as it is now constituted came about by careful planning.

The reverse is true....

A good illustration of the blighting tyranny of sanction is the present upheaval in the mining industry of Nova Scotia. We need coal for our railways, ships, industrial furnaces, and for our own comforts. We know that coal is taken from underground mines. We know that mines belong to certain companies. We know that workmen mine the coal and bring it to us. But not many know or question just how and why these mines belong to certain companies, who these companies are and were, how the wealth from the mines is made, how much the earnings are and should be, and who in reality is being advanced. Not many question or know who the workers are, what their conditions are and why, how much their earnings are or should be, and whether and how they are being advanced for serving us with coal.

A glance at the history of the mining industry, and at present conditions in the mine regions, tends to strengthen the belief that the conditions we have inherited so far have not come by careful direction, rather that they have happened through misdirection, and that if improvements are to come, habits and usage and present methods of work and relationship cannot and must not be accepted as unchanging and unchangeable laws.

The writer had the opportunity to visit Cape Breton this spring. She spent some time there while she delved into the history of the mining industry, and, by personal visitation she was able to observe closely the living and working conditions of the miners and their families.

Cape Breton's greatest wealth consists in its extensive and valuable mineral deposits. Carboniferous deposits cover about half of its whole area. The first regular mining of this vast coal area was started at Cow Bay by the French soldiers and laborers who were building the fortress at Louisburg.

By the middle of the eighteenth century, the Province of Nova Scotia changed from French to English ownership, and all the mineral lands were given by King George IV to his brother, the Duke of York. The Duke of York in turn leased them, in 1827 to the General Mining Association, a syndicate of joint stock companies, for an agreement that they were to pay off his debts, and to give him a share in the yearly profits. This marked the beginning of commercial coal mining in the province, for the G.M.A. with a capital investment of 274,690 pounds, installed engines for raising coal, pumping water, built workshops, erected a foundry, built a light railway to carry coal to the wharf, and imported miners from English colliery sections.

For fifteen years the G.M.A. controlled all the mineral lands in the province. But by 1845 a vigorous agitation began in the Provincial Assembly against the monopolistic hold of this syndicate. By 1858 the Province came into control, and the G.M.A surrendered their original lease, compensated the Duke, and secured in return from the Province, a long lease which gave them entire control and exclusive unmolestable rights to the coal areas in Cape Breton, Pictou County, Joggins and Springhill areas in Cumberland; their annual rent of 3,000 pounds was abolished, also the royalty on small coal. The G.M.A. opened and closed many mines, and in 1901 they sold out their mines in Pictou County to the N. S. Steel Co. for $1,000,000.

From 1858 to 1892 legislation actually existed which prohibited monopolistic holdings of coal areas, and as a result, 21 small companies sprang up in the province. But in 1892 Mr. H. M. Whitney, of Boston, made representations to the Government outlining the advantages that would accrue from a general consolidation of all coal mining companies. Aided by Premier Fielding, the Provincial Legislature amended the laws of N. S. so as to make the consolidation of mines possible. And that year Mr. Whitney applied for a charter of the Dominion Coal Company, which was formed by a syndicate of American and Canadian capitalists.

The Company was incorporated in 1893, with an authorized capital of $18,000,000. To assist the enterprise the Provincial government granted a lease for 99 years, to be renewed later for 20 years more; a subsidy of $3,200 per mile to build a railway from Sydney to Louisburg and a royalty of 12 1/2 cents per ton coal mined, was agreed upon, with a guarantee that same should not be increased.

By March 1st, 1895, the Company had acquired in full, some seventy miles of coal area, which had previously belonged under lease to the small companies. It has not been possible to discover what the capitalizations of the small companies were. But with the consolidated and authorized capital the Company began to put in coal cutting machinery; with the help of the government subsidy, it began to build the railway between Sydney and Louisburg.

The mines themselves are said to be of excellent quality, and the economic conditions incident to the operation of them favorable. The seams of coal are of great thickness, and their location near navigable waters, with direct and short water routes to markets, is a most important factor to the company's advantages.

With the economic conditions incident to the mining of coal favorable, with the installation of modern machinery, and with the increased facilities in transportation both by land and water, the output of the mines increased enormously, and the cost of production and transportation was reduced to a minimum. Additional markets now became necessary, and Mr. Whitney secured the Everett Coke and Gas Co. as one of the largest purchasers of the Dominion Coal Co. coal.

But so rapidly did the output of the mines increase that it became necessary for a larger industry to be supplied with coal. Meanwhile experiments proved that Cape Breton coal was well adapted for the manufacture of a good metallurgical coke. The idea then came to erect iron and steel works which would use the coke manufactured from the coal of the Dominion Coal Company's mines.

For the making of steel, limestone and iron ore are required. Cape Breton possesses limestone in great quantities. Iron ore is also to be found, but not to such a great extent. Newfoundland is rich in ore deposits. And Mr. Whitney was able to acquire a huge deposit of iron ore in Bell Island, Conception Bay, Newfoundland, from the Nova Scotia Steel Co., operating there.

Here it is interesting to pause and learn that the discovery of the existence of iron ore in Newfoundland came through a simple fisherman, who, in 1895 brought with him to Nova Scotia a huge block of hematite ore which he used as an anchor. Soon the Nova Scotia Steel Company Limited, for the modest sum of $120,000 acquired an area of, it is estimated, 35,000,000 tons easily accessible. In 1898 they sold a part of their concession to Mr. Whitney, for $1,000,000.

The formation of a large company to manufacture iron and steel in Cape Breton was largely assisted by the liberal bounties offered by the Dominion government. These bounties originated in 1882, when the Federal government began paying from $1.50 to $3.00 per ton bounty on all pig-iron and steel manufactured from Canadian ore and coal. In 1901 therefore, the Dominion Coal Co. issued a prospectus, asking for subscriptions for a large issue of stock, stating that they hoped to receive as bounty from the Dominion Government, a sum of not less than $8,000,000. To date the Company has received both from the Dominion and Provincial government in the form of bounties and subsidies, the amount of $90,000,000.

The Dominion Iron and Steel Co. Ltd., was chartered in 1898 by the legislature of N. S. with an authorized capital of $15,000,000. The charter gave the company extensive powers for mining, manufacturing, and transportation. It also empowered the municipal council to aid the enterprise by grants, and it authorized the town of Sydney to *exempt from town taxation, all property, income, and earnings of the company for a period of thirty years.* It also told the town to permit the Company to *expropriate any land it required and could not obtain by private treaty.*

The town of Sydney GAVE the Company their present site of four hundred and eighty acres of land, which was EXPROPRI-

ATED for the purpose, and a sum of $85,000 was VOTED to pay the appraisers. The Government of N. S. also agreed to remit to the Company fifty per cent of the royalty on coal consumed in the manufacture of steel, for a period of eight years.

The formation of the Dominion Steel and Iron works at Sydney created a vast market for the Dominion Coal Company, and in 1902 a lease was effected which made the two companies one.

Within twenty-five years the extent to which this company has entrenched itself in the province is miraculous. It powerfully controls and operates the mines on seventy square miles in Cape Breton. It owns and operates within each mine much and valuable machinery; it owns and controls the Sydney and Louisburg Railway, the Black Diamond Steamship Co., the Sydney and Louisburg piers, and the coal discharging towers at Montreal. It owns and lets out hundreds of houses to the mine workers; it owns in each mine district a large and heavily-stocked general store; it controls and exploits a large and valuable tract of iron ore deposits in Newfoundland, and dolomite and limestone quarries in Cape Breton. It owns and controls the immense iron and steel works in Sydney, with its coke ovens, blast furnaces, open hearth furnaces, mills, machine shops, electric plants, shipping piers, hundreds of workmen's dwellings, and it is free and untrammelled in its operations and habitation from provincial and local dictation and taxation.

For a period of thirty-six years, from 1884 to December 31st, 1920, the company's earnings were $33,307,329.96. The total dividends paid during the company's operations were $7,452,758.32. The balance of the earnings were put back into the property. The Company's annual statement shows that for the period ending 1921 they paid out on preferred shares, $5,350,000, and on common shares, $7,786,745. They laid away in reserve funds $9,500,000. Since then they have got from the Government $4,500,000 for a plate mill, and they now own both the mill and the money.

But the growth of the Company goes on. In 1920 representations were again made to the Government of N. S. portraying the further benefits that would result from a more comprehensive consolidation of the coal and steel industry in the province. The Dominion Government hesitated at the time, and finally refused to grant permission for what was clearly a monopolistic combine. But the Provincial Government, like an indulgent parent, lent a willing ear to its ambitious child, and helped create a new and more powerful body, which swept up the control of almost the entire mineral, steel and other economic resources of the province, by granting a charter to the British Empire Steel Corporation, Limited.

By the acquisition of the shares of the common stock, this corporation now controls the following constituent companies:

1. The Dominion Steel Corporation, Limited, which controls the following subsidiary companies: The Dominion Iron and Steel Co., Ltd.; The Dominion Coal Co., Ltd.; The Cumberland Railway Co., Ltd.; The Dominion Shipping Co., Ltd.; The Jas. Pender Co., Ltd.; The Sydney Lumber Co., Ltd.

2. The Nova Scotia Steel and Coal Co., Ltd.; which controls the following subsidiary companies: The Eastern Car Co., Ltd.; the Acadia Coal Co., Ltd.; The Wasis Steamship Co., Ltd.; The Nova Scotia Land Co.

3. The Halifax Shipyards, Limited.

The formation of the B.E.S. Co. was made possible by both the Provincial and Dominion Legislatures. The Provincial Legislature chartered the corporation under the Nova Scotia Companies' Act, and, on no clearly visible assets sufficient to warrant it, authorized the corporation to issue $500,000,000 in capital stock. For some reason, the company issued only $250,000,000 in capital stock. The Federal Government made this possible by failing to take the necessary steps, which would prohibit huge mergers to sew broadcast great amounts of watered stock, and on which shareholders "earn" huge dividends and bonuses on mythical assets.

The B.E.S. Co., among many others in this country is a glaring example—thus: At the merger the total issues of the component companies were: Common stock, $63,000,000; Preferred stock, $19,000,000. After the merger, the total issues of the component companies became, Common stock, $24,000,000; Preferred, $77,000,000. There was an actual watering of stock by the merger of *$19,000,000*, and thus water was moonshined into red wine! In addition to this, there has been an issue of $101,750,000 for, so far as evidence shows, purely a bonus distribution to the bondholders and to the parties promoting the merger. In addition to these bonuses and what not, the company pays its directors, men who know nothing of the practical end of the mining industry, and who are absentees of the province, and some of the country, yearly salaries ranging from $10,000 to $15,000 plus all travelling expenses, plus all final ownership in the buildings, machinery, railways, steamships, and other assets of the industry.

AND NOW LET US TURN to the other factor in the production of coal and steel, the workers. While it has been difficult for the writer to obtain information on early mining activities, it has been even more hard to obtain knowledge of the early miners and their fortunes. Tucked away in a negligible corner in an old discarded book the following scrap was found: —

The condition of the men was far from satisfactory in the Sydney Mines. In addition to their wages (and we are not told how much), they were given weekly rations of beef, pork, bread and molasses. The working time was from five a.m. to seven p.m. with an allowance of time (we are not told how much) for breakfast at seven a.m. and for dinner at one p.m. Before each meal a glass of raw rum was served to each man. At pay days, the men generally found, that after paying for their clothing, stores and rum, there were very small balances in their favor. The miners lived, ate and slept in two barracks or cook rooms; the sleeping berths being arranged in tiers alongside the rooms. Brawling and fighting were common.

Today (1925) Glace Bay, which contains the majority of the collieries, is considered to be the largest sized town in Canada. It contains about fourteen thousand families. Ten thousand are miners' families. Glace Bay now possesses one main street, two rows of shops on it, two movie houses, a Y.M.C.A. building, a post office, a tumble-down Town Hall, a single-track car line, a few electric lamp-posts, and about a half mile of sidewalk. Around this sidewalk with its lamp posts and street car and shops, live the towns-people — the merchants, doctors, and mine and town officials.

Social Worker Visits Cape Breton, 1925

About a quarter mile from the main street with its only side-walk and attractions, lie the colliery districts, where are encamped the ten thousand miners' families. Around each mine live the colony of workers employed in it. Each colliery section is near enough to the other to make up a compact town group.

Now, when a group of people congregate and form themselves into a town group with a town council, and work unceasingly for over thirty years to produce the wealth of their land, one expects to find at least the beginnings of civilized organized life, with its attendant comforts and culture. But in Glace Bay what do we find?

First of all there are no streets in any accepted meaning of the word. There are simply chunks of road, with rows and rows of wooden huts on either side. There are no sidewalks to mark off the ditches. There are no street lamps to light up the night darkness. No trees can grow in that soil, and a bit of green is a rarity. The scene then always is the dark, uneven, lumpy road, the rows of box-like huts, the mine tressel in the distance, smoke stacks, smoky skies, crude fencings, and rugged, stern, bare, sea cliffs. In the early spring it rains a good deal, and the atmosphere is clammy, foggy, drizzly, with raw, bitterly cold, ice-drift winds.

Second, the company owns the several hundred houses in which are housed the goodly several thousand miners' families. These houses were built cheaply and quickly, with a view to hurried, raw, camp life for bachelors. If these bachelors took wives unto themselves, and if children came to them, it is their lookout! Nobody cares. The houses are all of the same proportion, style and cheap lumber. Each house is of eight or nine rooms, divided by a thin wooden partition into two parts, and is called a "double" house. In each part of four rooms one or two families live, no matter how large. Each shack is a straight up-and-down affair, painted a dull slate color originally, and is now a muddy-dirt hue. On the inside the rooms are divided off by a single-coat of plaster or wooden wall, and give one a "jack-in-the-box" feeling of closeness. There are no porches; from the low wooden single doorstep, or no door-step, one walks in on the family to the kitchen or bedroom.

The houses are rarely repaired. If a miner wants his home to

73

look decent for his growing children, he buys paint and paper and the whole family set to work to decorate it. If the plaster crumbles, or if the floor cracks, it remains so for years. If a door breaks, or a window shatters, it is stuffed up with rags. If a chimney is broken, the family is smoked up for a time. If the walls, the floor or the windows are draughty, and the cold wind comes in, then the family simply catches cold. And so the writer witnessed countless homes, which remain dark and dismal, the plaster crumbling from walls and ceilings; the floors cracked and draughty; the windows low and stairways unsteady — children pale and coughing.

There are no bathrooms or running water facilities in the houses. The toilet is a dry box a few feet from the kitchen or bedroom. Few houses have electricity; when wanted, it is installed by the miner. Only in recent years have they been able to obtain tap water in the houses. The miner dug for it, and after due negotiations between the men and the company, the company refunded for the pipe used.

There are no provisions for sanitation; there are no drains or sewers in the colliery districts. Most of the homes have cesspools dug by the miner. Almost all have overflown, and everywhere one sees a lead pipe extending from the kitchen sink (made of tin or dishpan), and the sink refuse constantly flows into the front street or back yard ditch. When the rain comes, and it comes often near the sea, the ditch overflows, and the yellow-and-brown-mud road becomes impassably swollen, the empty lots around the mines, churches and school, where the children play, become miniature lakes. It is well-nigh summer before the rainfalls dry up.

For these accommodations the miner pays from $7.00 to $10.00 per month, with extra for water, coal and electricity, to the company.

There are two hospitals in Glace Bay with room only for one hundred and fifty patients. This accommodation for a community of fourteen thousand! And the splendid doctors, and the over-taxed nurses, with their sadly limited equipment, struggle bravely with the multitudes of pit accidents, with the births and illnesses galore.

There is no public health work of any organized nature done.

Social Worker Visits Cape Breton, 1925

Each hospital has a visiting nurse, who is sadly snowed under. As a result the condition of the children's teeth, eyes, throats and bodily growth, is shocking. The neglect of the general health of the men, women and babes goes without saying, and baby mortality is exceedingly high. A recent report on Tuberculosis in Canada shows that Nova Scotia ranks second highest in the extent of this scourge among its people.

There are four public schools; from fifty to sixty children are allotted to each teacher. Two of the schools have no central heating system. There are no school yards, and the children play in the empty lots around the mines, churches and stores. Of late some playthings, like swings, etc., have been brought in by some volunteers, and a small playground organized.

There are a goodly number of fine churches, representing the Catholic and Protestant denominations. Connected with these are social and recreation halls, built and run by parish funds.

Glace Bay has many merchants, who, in the course of years, have managed to reap fine harvests, to judge from their homes and living standards. The Dominion Coal Company, or now B.E.S. Co., has stationed in each mine section their general store, where the miners' families deal — but at prevailing Glace Bay prices, which are not free-town prices. At these stores, as at all local stores, credit is allowed. But this is no ordinary unprotected credit! This debt is collected weekly and inexorably from the envelope before it reaches the mine customer.

Here noteworthy mention must be made of the British-Canadian Co-operative Society, which operates a fine well-stocked store there, but to which only too few miners belong. The obvious reason is that few miners can scrape together sufficient money to buy a practical number of shares, and most of the time they are too deeply in debt at the company stores.

The above is a skeleton outline of the physical surroundings, the community organization and the material and cultural environment of the workers, the prime actors in the creation of Cape Breton's coal wealth.

And yet, if the workers would have steady work, every week, every year, the huge mass of them would go on managing to buy cheap, undernourishing food, cheap shoddy clothing, and making the best of their sullen-looking houses. They have never known and remain innocent of the pleasures which holidays, outing trips, good theatre, good music, libraries, and healthy social life can give. But the opportunity even to earn their crude camp existence is denied them. For, in the face of increased production and wealth, earnings for sheer life are denied them; or else work for a few days a week or month is dangled in front of them with a wage cut!

There are many theories extant on the "Law of Wages." Whatever theories may tell us, the facts are that somehow in the economic tangle, wages are paid just about or far below the costs of life-upkeep, the most obvious reason is that wages are a cost item to production, and are whittled down to the lowest possible minimum. Naturally, the man who receives wages, must, like one selling something, struggle vigorously for the best possible price. Unfortunately for us all, and for him in particular, the wage-receiver is selling himself, his labor-power, and so the struggle becomes one for the life and future of himself and loved ones. Like all merchants (but without the merchant dignity), the wage-earner's greatest blow comes when he has no market for his commodity, and hunger stalks in, robbing him of his stock.

It has not been possible to trace what the wages were in the early days of coal mining. But to-day, after a series of reductions, the datal or day-laborer at, around, and in the mines, receives from $2.60 to $4.05 per day. The coal cutter, or contractor, who does the most dangerous and skilled work, at the "face" of the coal seam, receives from $7.00 to $12.00 per day; but it must be noted that the latter works only a few days a week, since he can only cut as much as the datal man can take away. When these men work full time each week, they can earn in their different capacities, from $15.00 to $35.00 or $40.00 per week, or roughly, from $800 to $2,000 per year.

Knowing the average rates of wages, the writer found it of interest to gather figures on the cost of living in that region. She found, when pricing the "Health and Decency Standard" budget compiled and used by the U.S. Dept. of Labor, that if a worker there desires to keep himself and family on a decent health level, he requires to earn all the year round at least $31.08 per week, or $1,616 per year; and this budget makes no allowance for ordinary dental or special medical or hospital costs, for savings, or recreation.

Nine thousand out of the twelve thousand miners are day laborers. Less than half earn not more than at the highest rate, $4.00 per day, or $1,144 per year. More than half of these again, range from $780 to $1,000 per year, when working steadily. It is evident thus that even in the boom times, earnings do not allow them to live other than below, vastly below, the socially accepted "health and decency" standard.

Since the termination of the war, from whose battle-fields more than half of the stalwart Scotch-Canadian miners returned, all have had only one or two days per week, ten to twelve days work per month. This at the rate of $3.20 or even $7.00 per day! For five years they have borne slow starvation and nakedness. And yet this year again the company demanded a wage cut! Thanks to the organized strength of the workers, and to their splendid morale, they protested against this threatened invasion on their sparse earnings. The company in answer took their credit from them at the stores! It was work at OUR price or starve! And the men walked out of the mines, fighting for the dignity of their manhood and for the future of their homes, as they did, so gallantly, at Verdun.

After years of labor, with the curse of unemployment, high living costs, lowering wages, what has the miner achieved for himself? What future do his children face? How have they all benefitted by the increased production of coal and wealth? Let us look inside a datal mine-worker's "home."

A Scottish miner who had served for eighteen years in the coal pit, and for four years at the front, I found living with his family of wife and 8 children in the usual half of a company "double" house. Two rooms upstairs could not be used because of bad disrepair. The two downstairs served for bedroom and kitchen-livingroom. The plaster from the kitchen walls and half of the ceiling was crumbling, the floor humpy, but covered bravely with a home-made ragmat; the woodwork dirty, and for years unpainted. The cesspool has overflown, and refuse flows into the street. There are, of course, no sanitary conveniences, but there is a wire cord for an electric light. The furniture consists of a small cookstove, a deal table, four chairs, a wooden couch, a home-made kitchen cupboard. In the bedroom there are three beds, a rag mat. There is absolutely no bedding outside of two small pillows and a thin rag coverlet, and the mattresses are sagging and shedding cotton. For warmth the family go to bed in their clothing.

Not one of them have other clothing but what they wear. There is no change of underwear for anyone, and the children wear none at all; I found them in bed trying to keep warm, with thin cotton dresses against their little bare bodies. They had that winter not been to school or outdoors, for they had no boots or stockings. The miner, his wife and the older children have bad teeth and red defective eyes. The children have diseased throats and breathe badly. They all look undernourished; the children especially are wan, puny, with dark rings under their eyes. One little girl, three years of age, cannot yet walk — she still has rickets, and none for years have tasted cow's milk. It costs ten cents a pint in Glace Bay! The oldest boy, of 15, sells papers in the village in lieu of work in the mines. He has no boots; he was given that week a huge pair of lumberman's rubbers by the Relief Committee, together with an old coat.

And they have no food! They were half starved when the lock-out came, and now they live on the little food that the Relief Station gives, barely enough for two meals a day, every other day.

This miner, like hundreds or thousands of others, worked last year 173 days, at an average rate of $3.20 per day; totalling $553.60 for the year. His running expenses for the year are as follows:

House rent, at $7.00 per month	84.00
Coal	92.00
Sanitation (cleaning toilet box)	3.00
Light	28.80
Doctor, Hospital, Church, and other Relief	49.40
	$257.20

Social Worker Visits Cape Breton, 1925

The mine-worker must provide himself with pit clothes and other equipment, which costs as follows, yearly:

3 pairs of shoes, at $3.50	$10.50
4 suits of overalls, at $2.75	11.00
3 suits of underwear, at $2.00	6.00
5 pairs of sox, at 40 cents	2.00
1 cap, belt	1.00
Lunch cans	2.00
	$32.50

The total expenditure is, $289.70; his earnings for the year were $553.60; he had then $263.90 left for the year with which to provide all the necessaries of life, at the prices in his town, for himself, his wife and eight children, and also meet the many obligations of a citizen. Consequently the family has not bought any dry goods for that and three years' previous, and have starved. Besides that, years of future earnings, through debt, have been mortgaged merely to keep body and soul together.

With little variation these are the conditions to be found in every district in the mine regions of Cape Breton. Everywhere families are weighted down with heavy debt to the company and others, some to the amount of $600 and $800. Then there are those who have extra hospital debts, funeral debts, debts for births, for protracted illnesses, etc. For years they could think of nothing but how to get the food for the next day. Little wonder that they now are found starving, naked, and their homes bare!

For more than thirty years now there has been feverish activity in Cape Breton to exploit the mineral wealth there. The Dominion and the Provincial Governments, proud that we have these resources, have heaped up bounties and subsidies, amounting to date to $94,500,000 to companies adventuring in the ore fields. And through protective tariffs, through tax exemptions, and trade regulations, have assisted the successful growth of the iron and steel industry in Nova Scotia. The above figures and facts are inventory evidence that their efforts have been well rewarded; that the industry has grown to enormous proportions; and that a dozen or so individual directors, and other absentee shareholders and investors, have profited inordinately.

Magnificent Obsessions

But during the same number of years, several thousands of workers, investing their leisure, their lives and their limbs, have not had bounties, or subsidies, or tax exemptions offered them for encouragement; no material or cultural wealth has been accumulated; instead they now own — sickly, rickety, under-nourished children; anaemic, overworked wives, piles of debts, and do not own, but simply find shelter in homes with bare camp outfits, homes which offer no relief after the day's toil, homes which have no civilized standard of sanitation. There is nothing laid by in the form of clothing or bedding for the sake of health, let alone decency and pride of housekeeping. Life around them is drab, comfortless, unorganized. *Nobody has ever cared! Nobody cares!*

Legislators are the fathers of the people. The citizens of a country pay taxes, and the money is used intelligently and wisely by them for the betterment and development of the community.

In Nova Scotia, so far as the miners are concerned, this enlightened practice does not obtain. The physical surroundings of the miners are of the meanest and rudest; the proper development and future of the children unplanned and unprovided for; the investment of the citizen body is unprotected. But the people pay taxes, the province is being exploited, wealth is being produced. Where then does the money go? The answer is, to the Adventurers in the coal and ore fields. Again it may be asked, since the province is the basis and ultimate owner of the mineral resources, who then is the ultimate gainer from the production of its wealth? Again the answer is, THE ADVENTURER!

For it cannot be too often repeated, the Provincial and Federal Governments of Canada have not, and have declined, to use the taxpayer's money for the upbuilding of their people's communities, and for their relief when starving and in need, but they responded to the call for relief from the companies and poured out $94,500,000 to smooth their paths to wealth, protective laws were made at all times to ensure their progress.

At the time of writing the miners are still out of work. Their families are still starving. The Relief Committees which had been struggling valiantly till now with the problem of feeding the starving women and children from donations from citizens all over the country, have perforce ceased functioning. The miners' families are now trying to exist on the benefits paid by their Trade Union, whose funds do not allow for more than ninety cents per family per week! The Minister of Labor has recently returned from the region unsuccessful in his efforts to settle the dispute. The terms of the company to the workers were such as to bow them still lower in their misery and indignity, and, quite avowedly, an attempt to break their organization, which is their only protection. The mines are closed, production is at a complete standstill, but the pumping stations are manned by officials. During the last few weeks some hungry miners raided provision stores, and in their anger and misery tried to stop strike-breakers from going to work in the mines. The Dominion Government immediately dispatched troops to the mine regions to protect the property of the company, but did not send food to the children. The men undauntedly refuse to work for starvation wages, and the company, in the words of the President, Mr. Roy M. Wolvin, is "out to do its dirtiest." The Provincial Government so far as been helpless and ineffective in arbitrating a settlement with the company, for in April, the men were willing to go back to work at the 1924 wage scale.

Ofttimes a good guide to the future are the mistakes of the past. But the wise man is he who can face realities at all times. Now that the Party Government in Nova Scotia has changed, will the conditions of the workers be improved? Unquestionably NO!

A Royal Commission may be appointed, as so many others have been. It is doubtful, but some facts and figures may be gleaned of the Corporation's true financial state. It may even be conceded that the workers should not receive a wage cut. But as always, efforts, wordy efforts, will be made to keep them at the level where wages are never commensurate with the cost of life, while the company goes on its way receiving bounties, watering stock, inventing assets, and multiplying their unearned "earnings."

No. The Cape Breton tragedy and blight is not merely the result of party politics. It is a brilliant reflection of a system of production and distribution of the world's goods, which allows a group of men to trade on the vital needs of their brethren, and to use starvation as a weapon for obedience. Such a system is too deep-seated in its iniquity for dawdling, archaic, meaningless, party politics to cure. Neither the Conservatives with their Protectionism nor the Liberals with their traditional Free Trade, are the wise men. And where the welfare and justice for all depends upon who grabs and wields the vote, true Democracy is in danger, and as we now know it, is a farce....

We must shake ourselves free from the shackles that comfortable indifference and ignorance lay upon us. It is necessary, if we want fresh, free, glad life to continue, that we unhesitatingly probe into the history and the reason for the existence of every institution, every law, every custom and fixture of life in our midst. We must not take any habit or usage for granted. And above all, we must relate the existence of laws, of modes of life, and especially industrial and social powers, to the facts of social ill or well-being.

In the meantime let us be reminded that in a little corner of Canada, on the shore of the Atlantic, in Cape Breton, there are over *seventy thousand* (70,000) proud, Canadian Souls, who are at this very moment *starving, naked* and *pining away*. The writer appeals for HELP!

Sara M. Gold was a research worker for the Canadian Brotherhood of Railroad Employees, and this article was first published in *Social Welfare*, August-September, 1925.

8

The Pulp Mill
Comes to the Strait

I N 1952, WORK BEGAN on the construction of the Canso
Causeway. When completed, the Causeway would carry the
trains as well as automobiles, and put an end to the train ferries that crossed the Strait between Point Tupper and Mulgrave.
The train ferries were the economic base of those two communi-
ties, and without the ferries they were virtually finished. While the Causeway was being built, first Mulgrave and then the Four-County Development Association worked to bring a pulp mill as an alternative to economic disaster in the Strait area.

LEONARD O'NEIL, Mul-
grave: People get the idea
that we're asleep here.
They come down here and
take pictures of the empty
buildings. But at one time
here in Mulgrave we had

eleven stores, two doctors, a drug store and a druggist and a dentist. And we had our own hydro plant; we actually sold power to the Nova Scotia Power Company. And we worked here — the people did — to get the pulp mill in the Strait of Canso area.

EVA O'NEIL: The people here made their living from the Canadian National Railroad. When the Canso Causeway opened, that was the end — they were all unemployed. And the government did nothing for the people here.

LEONARD: They studied the rock in Cape Breton — they knew all about it — but they didn't know anything about what was going to happen to the people.

EVA: The men just got a notice they were through. This is a letter a deckhand on the Scotia got — they all got them:

As a result of the commencement of train service across the Causeway, our Strait of Canso Ferry Service will be discontinued 11:59 p.m.. May 14, 1955. I am obliged therefore to notify you that your employment with the Canadian National Railways will terminate at the close of business on the said date. It is regretted that at the said time, there is no other work with the railway which can be offered you.

LEONARD: And that was all the men received.

Some of them got work down in Yarmouth — not all of them — but they had to leave their homes. And they had a case of having to leave their families here, kids going to school, and go up there — because there was no possibility of even selling the house. The place went flat — Mulgrave went flat — and people couldn't give their homes away. They were tied down. It was a case of going somewhere else and renting, being separated from their families. It was a bump. And an awful lot didn't get work.

As mayor, I went to Angus L. Macdonald, premier of Nova Scotia — went for money to build a new school. Angus L. wanted to give $15,000 to fix up the old one, because he didn't know what would happen to Mulgrave.

So we went to work ourselves. I was out there when the great initial rocks were dumped, the start of the Causeway. A lot of people were saying, when they'd start dropping rock in there and a strong tide come, it would carry it out the Strait somewhere and they'd never finish it. But it kept on going, building across—and we knew it was coming.

So we had discussions, five or six of us in groups, we had discussions every evening. Five or six months, analyze the situation and wondering just what we might do, and we came up with the idea of the possibility of a pulp mill. I don't say the idea was original with me. If you look into the history of things—people that got the 99-year Oxford lease—they had agreed at that time, 1896, to build two pulp mills down here, one at the Strait and one at Baddeck. It was a 20-year lease with an option to renew it over a period of 99 years. When the first renewal came due, they were able to get the necessity of building one of the pulp mills eliminated. And during the course of renewals, they got all the requirements of a pulp mill eliminated.

Anyway, we held a special meeting of our town council. We agreed that a pulp mill would be a suitable thing for us to go after. We went down to Sydney to see Dr. Hugh Gillis and gave him the story and background, and he wrote it in good form and we got a brief printed. We sent out about 3000 of them to all levels of government, try to stimulate the government into some kind of action.

Mulgrave got off the first shot. It was later that we formed the Four-County Development Association (Richmond, Guysborough, Inverness, and Antigonish) to bring something to the Strait. But we knew this: that you can't tell a big industry where to locate. All you can hope for is to let them come and look at the site—the deep water, the harbour—and analyze the situation as far as water and all the other factors that go toward establishing an industry. We realized that, and for that reason we didn't say, "All right, we want the pulp mill in Mulgrave here"—although it would come to the Strait as a result of the water being on this side, only two miles over the hill here.

(*Do you mean that, the pulp mill that came to Point Tupper depends on water that comes from the Mulgrave side of the Strait?*) Yes. They had to have the water. It would take 35,000 gallons of water to process one ton of pulp. And there's 20 million gallons of water going across the Strait every day, to run that mill—and it's going across from the lakes back of Mulgrave. It's piped under the Strait—a 23-inch pipe—over to the pulp mill. (*They're not getting it from the Port Hawkesbury side?*) No. There's a high mineral content in the water over there, which would require expensive filtration. There's suitable water over here.

There was so much involved. You'd hardly believe all the work. Believe it or not, there were people trying to stop the pulp mill from coming to the Strait. Why would they do that? Well, because crown lands were a great thing for a government in power to have, to feed a little bit to their friends, in leases. They'd get a lease on so much land, cut the pulp off it, and sell the pulp. Even as far away as British Columbia and up in Quebec—an unwritten agreement amongst the companies in New Brunswick and Quebec that they would not enter the field down here. It was a very convenient place for them to come—not every year, perhaps every second or third year—come into this area and set up a very, very good price for the pulp for the people who would go in and get it out and load it on a boat here, take it up to the mills in Quebec. You'd say, why did they do that? When they'd get a bad winter up there, they couldn't get their stuff out—too much snow or too mild a winter, bad winter for operating in the woods—it was better for them to come out here and pay a bigger price for the wood and then get out of here, rather than raise the prices up there to encourage woodlot owners to bring wood out. Because once they got it up, then the woodlot owners wouldn't want to sell again at a low price. That was the reasoning behind that. And that's a fact. So those people didn't want a pulp mill here.

And there were interests that didn't want the Stora Koppaberg to come in here because it was a Swedish concern with a special patent on wood processing. And they knew they couldn't compete with them—and they can't compete with them. And then there's this: a great number of people in politics were also involved in the lumber business. And you see, there are two types of mentality in the forest: the longstick—that's the man that's interested in lumber, you know, logs—and the people that are interested in pulp—and the people that are interested in logs don't like to see pulp cut because it's a tree that's not fully developed, not the full potential there. It takes 50 years to get a log, pulp about 25, and you have a market for it.

(*Let me understand: the government was fighting you, not on where it should be located, but against having a pulp mill at all?*) Absolutely. (*And it became an issue during the 1956 election.*) When they saw it was going to be a popular thing, the Liberals were building them all over the place.

From Leonard O'Neil's notes at that time:

In the '56 election campaign, Henry Hicks, Collie Chisholm, and Clyde Nunn opened the campaign at some kind of club outside Halifax. Hicks told the audience of a 35-million-dollar mill for Sheet Harbour. A few nights later... he assured them of a mill for Pictou County. The next night at a meeting at Lower South River, he spoke of a 35-million-dollar mill further east. The next afternoon he told of a 40-million-dollar mill for Guysborough County.

Henry Hicks promised five pulp mills altogether between Halifax and down here. Even promised one for here.

I had been chairman of the Liberal Association—but I'm no longer a Liberal, since they bucked us on the pulp mill. See, Angus L. Macdonald had been premier. I'll tell you about Angus L. He often went back and forth to his home down there in Cape Breton. He'd often drop into my garage, sit down and eat peanuts and talk. The day the Causeway started—the first load of rock dumped—he came with Chevrier, Federal Minister of Transport, to a joint meeting in Mulgrave of the Port Hawkesbury Board of Trade and the Mulgrave Board of Trade. We outlined our concerns, the men here losing their jobs. Chevrier's reaction was that it was purely a local problem. But Angus L. said, "No, it isn't purely local. These people are working people. They don't have funds to enter into alternate forms of industry or employment. We've got to do something about it." Then shortly after that, he got sick and I sent ten dollars to his secretary to get a bouquet of flowers for him, and the ten dollars was used to buy a mass card for him—he died. And that brought on the appointment of Henry Hicks as premier of Nova Scotia in 1954. And that stopped things there. I've always thought and always said, if Angus L. Macdonald had stayed in, that we wouldn't have run into the same problems and made faster progress to the pulp mill.

Anyhow, wood. That was something we had that was natural to us. And we had the water. We *felt* that we had water. We had a meeting in Antigonish—people came from all over. I was in the garage business. Anyone came in the garage to buy a car, I talked pulp mill with them. It gets in your blood. I knew the possibilities were there, and I don't know what was driving me on. All the time. I'd go up there 5 o'clock in the morning and look over the area. You become possessed with the idea till you can't let go. I wouldn't let go regardless of what happened. Once the Causeway opened, the business that I had went down to nothing because there was no traffic by here. People were all out of work. I had the old sheriff here more than once at the door.

EVA: Even came to turn our lights out, take out our phone— that's how hard we had it. (*This place got hit....*) Boy, did it ever. You don't know the half of it. Leonard had to go to Halifax to work finally. I was here alone with the kids, he'd come home on the week- ends. He worked 13 years away. I brought the kids up alone.

LEONARD: Back to the water again. At the big meeting in Antigonish, two of the cabinet ministers—one represented us here and the other was Minister of Lands and Forests—during the meeting one got up and said they had had a private firm come in and look the site over here, that there was a company interested in building a pulp mill, but that the company needed 12 million gallons of water—but that we here had only 9 million gallons of water, so there was no possibility of getting a pulp mill. The other cabinet minister stood up and put his shoulders back and said, "Ladies and gentlemen, 12 million gallons is a lot of water," and he sat down. That's all he said.

So I got up—the auditorium in Antigonish was full—and I said, "Ladies and gentlemen"—maybe I wasn't that polite—but I said, "we have got the water, and I can prove it." Cripes, there was damn near a riot in the auditorium. People seemed to believe me and thought someone was trying to sell us down the river. Cripes, some of the women were crying, everyone was just mad- der than a hatter.

EVA: You see, that meeting in Antigonish condemned the site. They said we didn't have enough water. And if we had failed there, there would have been no pulp mill anywhere in the Strait area. That's for sure.

LEONARD: The reason I knew it wasn't true — them saying we only had 9 when it required 12 — because when this thing started, I went to Halifax to see how much water we did have. And three of the lakes back two miles had a river coming from them, and they were tapped into a hydro plant that Mulgrave owned there for a number of years. And I found out they were using 12 million gallons a day there. So I told the meeting, the ministers were wrong and I could prove it. Well, the fat was in the fire after that. And that was just that one set of lakes, and we had more — we had plenty of water. After that night in Antigonish, one of the ministers called up, said he'd never go to one of those meetings again. I said, "You'll never get asked, as far as I'm concerned."

Robert Winters was the federal Member, and he was a pretty good friend of mine. I called him and I called one of the provincial Members — I don't remember which — and I told them that I wasn't satisfied with that meeting, that we did have the water — their own records in Halifax showed that we had what was needed, and more on the Barry Lake, and that didn't include Goose Harbour. The information I had on Goose Harbour was that there was 16 million gallons of water there. So I told the government, unless we get this thing straightened away properly and aboveboard, I'm going to the papers with everything I have. I wanted to deal more openly with the whole situation. In about a week's time, I got a call from Halifax. They were sending down a hydro engineer. Would I be free to go out with him to the lakes?

Some of us went out. This engineer said, "You can't dam this place. The water is running out." But we were convinced this fellow was wrong, because he never got out of the boat. I got suspicious. Normally I would have believed him, but something told me not to. I went down there — and I saw right away what had confused him. The trees at the edge of the lake were taller, getting more moisture, while the other ones were shrub. And sitting in the boat, it looked as though the land dropped away — but it was just the top of the trees, the land raised behind there. I called up, lied a little bit, said we had two surveyors out there—that place can be dammed.

So they sent an engineer down and we all went out Goose Harbour Lake. We started away in the morning, bright and early, surveyed—including John Randall, Montreal Engineering. Took us the day. Just about 5 o'clock when we finished. I was so tired I didn't know whether I'd walk out of there or not. "John," I said, "I want you to tell me whether you can dam that or not. And if you can't, I'm going to stay here." He figured for a while and said, "Yes, you can put a 20-foot dam on that. And before we came out here, I looked at the watershed area—and there's something like 16 million gallons of water." Now that's how close we came to not getting the pulp mill.

Because really, the government sent Montreal Engineering in to prove that I was wrong. But it turned out I was right. There was enough water. And that's why water goes from this side of the Strait over to the pulp mill.

I had hoped that the mill would be here in Mulgrave. In fact, here's what our plan was at that time. Dr. Don MacNeil and I went to Halifax to meet members of the British American Oil Company. And we took out a map of Nova Scotia and penciled out the Point Tupper area and suggested that as an ideal place for an oil refinery. And we thought without any question that the pulp mill was coming on this side, so we'd have employment on both sides of the Strait. This is the way we were looking at it.

There was still the problem of assuring any prospective company they would have enough wood. There was about 1 million acres of crown land. And there were several leases. The Oxford Paper Company had 35,000 acres in Cape Breton on a long-term lease. The balance, about 50%, was held for the most part by small woodlot owners in the eastern counties. One of the things to bring any company in, the Oxford lease to the crown—the crown had to get title to it because no company would come in here with 50% of the wood owned by these small woodlot owners. If a company comes in here and they spend 40 million dollars, the thing they are concerned with is the supply of wood, the raw material. Now, if 50% of it is in the hands of small woodlot owners, well, what's to stop these small woodlot owners from saying they want more a cord—"You've got to give it to us or you can't get your wood." For that reason, no company would risk that amount of capital in here on an open market of that kind.

Stora Koppaberg had expressed interest to Hicks's government but could not get assurance that they would get the wood. Then Hicks's government was defeated in that 1956 election, and Stanfield came into the picture. We went to see him and explained everything. Couldn't give us any answer at all. The next time we went in there—a month's time—he had put an awful lot of study in it and knew the thing inside out. He said then, in the best interest of Nova Scotia, the Oxford lease should be reconvened to the crown. That would give the pulp company enough crown land wood to operate almost independently from the small woodlot owners if the small woodlot owners would decide they wouldn't sell to them. And I knew then we were going to get the pulp mill.

(*One thing I don't understand: after the water was found here, why did the pulp mill go to the Port Hawkesbury side?*)

I saw the plan. I worked with Simon Engineers who were doing the site location work. I went to work with them to get closer—85 cents an hour. One morning the engineer came over to me and said, "Well, we made a final decision last night. The mill is coming to Mulgrave, and I'm glad," he said, "because you people need it the most." It was to be down at Pirate Harbour—the lower end of town. That was all to be filled in and that was the site for it. (*It was that definite?*) H. J. Rice, the former mayor of Canso, wrote to me: "The broadcast by Premier Stanfield at noon today and the fuller announcement in the *Chronicle-Herald* received tonight re the pulp mill in the Mulgrave area is indeed good news."

Still, we were leery. We knew companies were buying land on the Port Hawkesbury side. Simon's Engineering recommended for here. Karl Clauson was the president of the Nova Scotia Pulp Company as it was set up first, and he brought Charles T. Maine and Company in for further recommendation—and they said to put it on the other side because they had more land over there. It was a combination of things. A great hue and cry that things were tough in Cape Breton, the mines, a lot being laid off. Minister of Trade and Industry was from Sydney, and they would have had to buy 28 homes in Mulgrave if they built on this side—a combination of these things, I think. And once the company got permission from the government to take the water from here across the Strait, then the rest fell in place.

But where it went doesn't make too much difference. A lot of people from this side get work over there. And we get a fair amount of taxes from all that industry over there—it's split up for the area generally. It doesn't all go to Hawkesbury. Point blank now, I can say that I'm happy that it went over there. If that mill was in town here, we'd have to leave our homes for the smell of it. Take 28 homes and that would bring it halfway up the town. And what's happening today in what is left of Point Tupper could have happened here. [At that time, the Point Tupper community was into Phase Four of a program of relocation.]

The Causeway created the deep-water harbour, and the first recognition of its value was the Nova Scotia Pulp Company—the first major industry to come to Nova Scotia in 25 years.

The Opening Day of the Canso Causeway, 1955.

9

The Four Lives of the Mi'kmaw Copper Pot

Calvin Martin

TWO YEARS AFTER HIS RETURN HOME to France, in 1614, the French Jesuit Pierre Biard set down his memoirs of three stormy years spent in Acadia. A bitter man who had been ill-used by the commandant at Port-Royal, Charles de Biencourt, Biard's relation is clearly self-serving. Nonetheless, despite this blemish, it remains

While digging a sewer line in 1955, Ken Hopps of Pictou came across 22 copper pots.

an extremely valuable commentary on early Indian and white relations. Contained within its sparse prose, for instance, we find a list of goods which were customarily exchanges in the early seventeenth-century trade between the two ethnic groups. "All this new France is divided into different tribes," he intoned, "each one having its own separate language and country. They assemble in the Summer to trade with us, principally at the great river [St. Lawrence]. To this place come also several other tribes from afar off. They barter their skins of beaver, otter, deer, marten, seal, etc., for bread, peas, beans, prunes, tobacco, etc.; kettles, hatchets, iron arrowpoints, awls, puncheons, cloaks, blankets, and all other such commodities as the French bring them."

Beguiling in its dryness, this abbreviated catalog was in a reality the living anatomy of one of the most revolutionary institutions in North American contact history. What in pre-Columbian times had been a non-profit, balanced, reciprocal exchange of necessities and luxuries between Northeastern and Eastern Subarctic tribes and bands was completely overhauled in historic times into a highly competitive, individualistic, profit-oriented enterprise centered on the furs and skins of furbearing species and large herbivores. In its wake, natives resorted to technological eclecticism as they selectively adopted European tools and techniques, adding them to their existing inventory; male Indians began emerging as an unprecedented merchant class, shifting the locus of authority in matrilineal clan societies like that of the Huron; and intertribal rivalries ominously gathered momentum, leading to confederations of tribes for mutual security.

Aboriginal society in many instances became seasonally atomized (e.g. as families ranged over winter hunting territories), and aboriginal culture, under pressure from the trade, disease, and missionization, was rendered increasingly dysfunctional. Across the board, the Indian way of life was being shaken in a most profound sense. In the economic sphere, the Indian's focus of subsistence was no longer based on the food quest; now most of his foraging energies were directed toward supplying an insatiable, extramural demand for furs. The vicious cycle of dependency which was thereby set in motion eventually castrated the native

subsistence economy, reducing numerous heads of families to debt peonage.

And it all started with a few, seemingly innocuous trade goods: greased and "dry" beaver pelts, together with the furs and skins of lesser rodents and browsers, bartered for European hardware, foodstuffs, and raiment. The Jesuit's inventory is clearly misleadin[g] French items he so casual[ly] implications for the aborig[inal]

An iron-handled, open copper kettle measuring twenty-five inches across and thirteen inches deep strikes us as a fairly prosaic item of exchange, but to the Mi'kmaq of the Canadian Maritime provinces it was "the most valuable article they can obtain from us." So declared the seventeenth-century Acadian merchant, Nicolas Denys, who underscored his point with an anecdote of a Mi'kmaw who was allegedly conducted on a grand tour of Paris. What clearly impressed him above all else were the coppersmiths who forged those marvelous kettles. Surely, he is said to have exclaimed, these artisans were relatives of the French monarch!

What Denys meant was that the kettle was more to these people than simply a handy cooking vessel. Much more than that, we know that it was an instrument which pervaded the exchange economy (as a highly-prized commodity of trade), the ceremonial complex (as grave furniture, for instance), the overarching belief system (like all other material culture, it was invested with an animating spirit), and, lastly, the settlement pattern (to the degree that it contributed to the overthrow of wooden-cauldron-based territories). There is nothing remarkable about the first revelation—the copper-kettle-as-commodity idea. We would expect as much. Moreover, those among us who are familiar with Northeastern ethnology and historic archaeology are aware of the spiritual (which includes ceremonial) role these trade goods came to have in native society. For these reasons, the first three kettle functions—commodity, grave furniture, and spiritual identity—will be given brief notice. It is the last function, the demographic function, which is novel to this study, and accordingly calls for extended commentary.

After forty years of trafficking with the Acadian Indians, from 1632 to 1672, the aging Denys could write categorically that "the things which come from us...(have) become to them an indispensable necessity. They have abandoned all their own utensils," he wrote in the late 1660s, "whether because of the trouble they had as well to make as to use them, or because of the facility of obtaining from us, in exchange for skins which cost them almost nothing, the things which seemed to them invaluable, not so much for their novelty as for the convenience they derived therefrom." The brisk trade in kettles he was alluding to owed its longevity and volume to various siphoning-off processes which included, along with breakage and loss, a secondary trade with New England tribesmen. Thus Marc Lescarbot reported the Mi'kmaw sagamore, Messamoet, peddling "kettles, large, medium, and small, hatchets, knives, dresses, capes, red jackets, peas, beans, biscuits, and other such things" among the Saco River Algonkians, for which he was given corn, tobacco, beans, and pumpkins—plant domesticants which the Mi'kmaq were either unable or not inclined to grow.

Another force behind this persistent, cumulative demand was the need to replace kettles that had been buried as ceremonial objects along with the human deceased. There were, in truth, few Indian customs which exercised the French as much as this one did. After a year spent outdoors on a scaffold, wrapped in a birch-bark sheet, the dead had their bones gathered up and "placed in a new coffin or bier, also of Birch bark, and immediately after in a deep grave which they [the bereaved] had made in the ground." From Chrestien Le Clercq, whose twelve-year ministry (1675-1687) among the Mi'kmaq of the Gaspé Peninsula brought him into contact with a slightly different clientele than Denys, we learn of primary burials. Upon death, disclosed the Recollet, corpses were immediately interred in a circular grave in a flexed position, following which the relatives and friends "bury...everything which these possessed while on the earth, in the belief that each article in particular renders them the same service in the Land of Souls that it did to its owner when alive." Denys saw graveside mourners toss in "bows, arrows, snow-shoes, spears, robes of Moose, Otter, and Beaver, stockings, moccasins, and everything that was needful for him in hunting and in clothing himself... At a time when they were not yet disabused of their errors, I have seen them give to the dead man, guns, axes, iron arrow-heads, and kettles, for they held all these to be much more convenient for their use than would have been their kettles of wood, their axes of stone, and their knives of bone, for their use in the other world." To which he appended, ruefully, "there have been dead men in my time who have taken away more than two thousand pounds of peltries."

One can imagine the dismay of these Frenchmen as they stood by watching the dirt being heaped over these previous pelts. What an utter waste, it must have seemed to them. In the early years, whenever they remonstrated with the Indians for this folly, they were rebuffed, "although they have been told that all these things perished in the earth, and that if they would look there they would see that nothing had gone with the dead man." So insistent were the French that one gamy Indian, at least, agreed to accept the taunt. Opening a grave, he started sifting through the decayed furniture when he came upon a badly oxidized copper kettle, which he snatched up and tapped. Finding "that it no longer sounded, [he] began to make a great cry, and said that some one wished to deceive them. 'We see indeed,' said he, 'the robes and all the rest, and if they are still there it is a sign that the dead man has not had need of them in the other world, where they have enough of them because of the length of time that they have been furnished with them... But with respect to the kettle,' said he, 'they [the deceased] have need of it, since it is among us a utensil of new introduction, and with which the other world cannot [yet] be furnished. Do you not indeed see,' said he, rapping again on the kettle, 'that it has no longer any sound, and that it no longer says a word, because its spirit has abandoned it to go to be of use in the other world to the dead man to whom we have given it?'" Denys and his cronies thought this was hilarious, and rejoined by presenting the man with an old, worn-out kettle that turned out to be just as dumb as the first one. Convinced that they had now stumped him, they challenged him to explain the apparent discrepancy. "'Ha,' said he, 'that is because it is dead, and its soul has gone to the land where the souls of kettles are accustomed to go.' And no other reason could be given at that time," reported Denys in apparent disgust.

The Indian, for his part, was probably just as frustrated at the stupidity of the French, on whom he had wasted a brief lesson in the concept of "soul loss," a common belief among North American Indians. According to this view, an object died upon being deprived of its soul, usually by means of sorcery. Soulless people and material objects continued to function or look alive, as the case may be, but in reality they were dead. Indians often attributed illness to soul deprivation and engaged shamans to retrieve the errant member. Evidently copper kettles became dumb and no longer rang when tapped where bereft of their spirits; likewise, broken canoes "and all other things out of service" were considered "dead" by the Mi'kmaq. Clearly there was nothing misleading or disingenuous in the Indian's exposition. Yet it was all for naught. Denys and his friends may have lost a battle, but ultimately they won the war. "Nevertheless," he later confided, "they have been disabused of that in the end, though with much difficulty."

We are fortunate in being able to check the details of Denys' description of seventeenth-century Mi'kmaq mortuary customs against the archaeological record, and to his credit Denys has been confirmed as a remarkably perceptive ethnographer. So concluded J. Russell Harper in a report on two mid-seventeenth-century Mi'kmaq burial sites he excavated in the vicinity of Pictou Harbour, Nova Scotia, in the mid 1950s. Both pits were circular (notice Le Clercq's statement to the same effect), measuring roughly six feet across by three feet deep. The floor of one of the pits, Burial Pit No. 1 in Harper's report, was strewn with twigs and branches, over which was a layer of birchbark reaching about a foot and a half up the sides. Evidence of red ocher on the bark testified to the spiritual potency of the setting. "Five layers of pelts lay above the bark on the floor"—the pelts that Denys and his cohorts so impiously mourned. "Three intact inverted copper kettles lay on the painted skin [i.e., the top pelt with flesh side up, painted red]. Beneath each kettle was a very black layer of decayed organic material." Very likely this was all that remained of a food offering to the spirit of the deceased. Harper went on to enumerate the grave gifts which were found beneath the kettles: a bow, a hafted iron axe, awls, bits of cloth, "and a glazed pottery beaker." Curiously, a "moose skin covered Kettles Nos. 1 and 3, and a black bear skin, hair side down, covered Kettle No. 2." Some artifacts had been placed between the kettles, somewhat filling the interstices. Afterwards, when all was in place, "earth had been added until the kettles were covered, then a birch bark sheet laid over the fill at a depth of 1 1/2 feet from the grave floor" with evidence of the lower and upper sheets having been stitched together to form a tidy envelope. Finally, earth and stone fill were heaped over the carefully prepared bundle. Somewhat perplexingly, there was an extension of this primary pit—a "much less carefully prepared" cyst—that was evidently added onto the other at a somewhat later date. Each of the four kettles in this annex was "mutilated; some were badly crushed by deliberate flattening under heavy pressure [jumped on?], and the balance were slashed with an axe. All had been evidently 'killed' to release the spirit of the dead at burial."

Harper excavated a similar burial complex the following year, 1956, where he found two layers of bodies. The lowest stratum contained a profusion of both French trade goods and native handicrafts. Of the former, several kettles had been "crushed or completely smashed" to form an under sheet, upon which were axes, chisels, scrapers, spears "and other French iron material," strung beads, and two woolen blankets. Reed baskets, rush matting, a birchbark dish, fragments of a wooden box, the usual birchbark sheets, and a stack of pelts (deer, moose, bear, and squirrel) comprised the aboriginal contribution.

Immediately above this Harper excavated another burial: an inverted copper kettle shielding a skull and several long bones, adjoining a second kettle "wrapped snugly in sewn birch bark sheeting" placed over a small pile of what had once been food. The impression one gets is that some kettles were spared mutilation in order to serve as a protective shield for grave goods and the bones of the deceased, while others were ripped apart so as to sheathe the grave floor with metal, while still others were ceremonially slain to provide the spirit of the deceased with the spirit of this most useful vessel in the afterlife. Yet such "foolish fancy," as Le Clercq uncharitably put it, came to an end in the latter quarter of the century.

But a kettle, like a cat, has several lives — in this case four. As well as being a commodity of exchange and a cherished cooking vessel, a popular piece of grave furniture, and an interloper in the Mi'kmaw pantheon of spirits, the copper kettle served in addition a geographical-social function: it contributed to the dissolution of the traditional mode of settlement and, more ambiguously, land tenure...

The earliest archaeological evidence on these Indians, presumably Mi'kmaw, seems to indicate that they occupied coastal fishing and shellfishing campsites year-round. Naturally, we have no conception of their mode of land tenure at this early date. Evidently sometime in the late twelfth century, perhaps in response to a marked climatic cooling in the North Atlantic, this pattern shifted: winters were thereafter spent in the interior. Something comparable to this occurred in central and eastern Maine in late prehistoric-protohistoric times, writes the Maine archaeologist Bruce J. Bourque. An examination of three coastal sites disclosed that their inhabitants were occupying the coast during the late winter and early spring (March through May), whereas historic records show that by 1550 Maine Indians were passing this quarter hunting, trapping, and fishing in the interior. Bourque contemplates two viable explanations for this turn-about: either it was due to the so-called Little Ice Age, just referred to, or it is indicative of a decision to participate in a remarkably precocious European fur trade.

Significantly, these Maine Indians were visiting the coast in the late spring, summer, and early fall (June through September), precisely the time when European fishing fleets were codfishing and whaling in coastal Atlantic waters. Fur trade historians have traditionally dated the beginning of the Atlantic coastal trade no earlier than 1500 or so, shortly after English, Norman, Basque, and Portuguese fishing fleets began making regular, annual runs to the Grand Banks. Records show that these fishermen were the first to barter with the coastal tribes and bands, presumably in the course of drying and salting their catch on the rocky shores and inlets of Labrador and eastern Newfoundland. What was thus begun as a casual exchange of trinkets and other wares for a few pelts quickly became a booming industry in the early seventeenth century, following a late sixteenth-century take-off in the European hatting business.

On the basis of this somewhat contradictory evidence it is difficult to imagine why twelfth-century Mi'kmaq Indians would have revised their settlement habits from winters spent clamming on the seacoast to winters spent hunting inland by invoking the commercial fur trade hypothesis. For there seems to be a discrepancy here of 300 years between the adoption of one and the inauguration of the other. Either our date is in error, and this shift happened several centuries later, in alignment with the earliest fur trade impulse, or there were indeed climatic or other reasons (perhaps Norse influences) responsible for this anomaly. Regardless of the exact date, it would make sense, of course, for early sixteenth-century Mi'kmaq band segments or families—we are unclear which was the basic hunting group at this early contact date—to hunt beaver and other furbearers, caribou, and moose in the interior during the height of winter, for this is when their pelts and skins are in their prime. It was also the logical time for the snowshoed hunter to prey on the large herbivores rendered helpless by the deep March snows.

In his *Histoire de la Nouvelle-France*, published in 1609, Marc Lescarbot confirmed that the Mi'kmaq of his time were adhering to a seasonal migration cycle similar to that of their southern brethren, the Maine Wabanaki described by Bourque. Despite a brief residency in Acadia—barely over a year, from 1606 to 1607—Lescarbot proved to be a respectable ethnographer. The Mi'kmaq preferred to conduct their hunting during the winter season, he explained, "when the fish withdraw" from the coast—"feeling the cold," as he quaintly phrased it. There was no need for them to retire into the interior during the other three seasons as these fish, a dietary staple, were sufficient to their needs. Only in the winter did

> the savages forsake the sea-shores and encamp in the woods, wherever they know that there is any prey... In the countries where there are beavers, as throughout all the great river of Canada, and upon the coasts of the ocean as far as the country of the Armouchiquois (New England Wabanaki), they winter upon the shores of the lakes, to catch the said beavers."

This final emphasis on the beaver was, of course, an oblique reference to the animal's worth in the fur trade.

Pierre Biard, more explicit than Lescarbot, described a similar seasonal pattern: winters spent inland and the remainder of the year passed at the coast. From mid-September into October, the Mi'kmaq migrated inland, above the tidal zone, to the "little rivers" where the eels were spawning. For the rest of the month and all of November they concentrated on hunting beaver and "elks" (caribou?). Tomcod and young turtles were harvested throughout December. Disregarding January for a moment, Biard designated February to mid-March as the principal season for the beaver, otter, moose, woodland caribou, and bear hunt. Beginning in mid-March, anadromous fish (first smelt, soon followed by herring) and northward-migrating wildfowl occupied their attention. And as the spring unfolded these were supplemented by sturgeon, salmon, and innumerable birds' eggs. The period from May to mid-September was the flush season: cod and other fish, along with shellfish and French trade goods (including food) provided a broad margin of security. Finally, as autumn approached, everyone prepared to move into the interior once more....

It is the injection of French trade goods into this seasonal rhythm which especially interests us. Undoubtedly, one of the very earliest items bartered in the Atlantic coastal trade was the metal kettle. Historic archaeological investigations at coastal and interior sites have revealed that until the early seventeenth century, brass kettles at least were routinely cut up and fashioned into body ornaments or utilitarian objects; initially, it would seem coastal Algonkian tribes had little inclination to use them as cooking vessels. So, too, did the protohistoric Wabanaki dispose of their copper pots. Whatever their earlier preferences, we know that by the beginning of the seventeenth century the Mi'kmaq were accustomed to boiling their food in their shiny French kettles.

Acknowledged Lescarbot: "In the countries where they use tillage, as in that of the Armouchiquois, and farther and farther off, the men make earthen pots, in the shape of a nightcap, in which they seethe their meats, flesh, fish, beans, corn, squashes, etc. Our Souriquois [Mi'kmaq] formerly did the same, and tilled the ground; but since the French bring them kettles, beans, peas, biscuit, and other food, they are become slothful, and make no more account of those exercises."

Archaeologists doubt Lescarbot's claim (and Le Clercq's intimation) that the prehistoric Mi'kmaq once farmed; there is nothing in the archaeological record which would suggest they did. The absence of milling tools is rather conspicuous. As for the ceramic pots referred to by Lescarbot, we have overwhelming evidence in the form of numerous sherds recovered from coastal and interior middens that Indians living here in prehistoric times were pottery-makers. The question is, who were these ceramicists and when did they ply their craft?

There is no assurance that these potters were Mi'kmaq. Surely these prehistoric Mi'kmaq had some better, more capacious, way of preparing their food (than clay pots or sewn birchbark).

In his brief Mi'kmaw vocabulary, Marc Lescarbot furnished a clue as to what this was. Reading down the list of native words, with their French (English-translated) equivalents, one discovers that Lescarbot made a curious distinction between a "cauldron" and a "platter, or dish." The Mi'kmaw word for the former was "aouau, or astikov"; the word for "dish" (as in birchbark dish, described above) was "ouragan." What, exactly, was the nature of this cauldron? Silas Rand's celebrated English-Mi'kmaq dictionary contains what appears to be a phonetic variant of the noun in its verb form: "A trough, Wolsaktaoo." In translation, "Wolsaktaoo" means "I hew it out forming a trough or a 'dugout.'" In another context Lescarbot provided a graphic description of this "aouau" when he discussed the manner in which he and some Indian companions had an impromptu feast of moose one winter's day. "After the roast we had boiled meat, and broth abundantly, made ready in an instant by a savage, who framed with his hatchet a tub or trough of the trunk of a tree, in which he boiled the flesh. His manner of doing so was a thing which I have admired, and which when I put the question to them, many who think they have good wits could not think out. Yet it is but simple, being to put in the said trough stones made red hot in the fire and to renew them until the meat is boiled."

We turn to Nicolas Denys for an ample description of this novel culinary device. "Before speaking of the way they live at present," he advises the reader, "it is necessary to look into the past. Their subsistence was of fish and meat roasted and boiled." Roasting was done either by spitting the meat and exposing it to the flames, or by spitting it in such a way that it slowly rotated before the fire, or by placing the flesh directly in the coals. Fish was either grilled or broiled in the coals, great care being taken to insure that it was thoroughly cooked before being eaten. But the main course was yet to come.

The Four Lives of the Mi'kmaw Copper Pot

All these kinds of roasts were only an entree to arouse the appetite; in another place was the kettle, which was boiling. This kettle was of wood, made like a huge feeding-trough or stone watering-trough. To make it they took the butt of a huge tree which had fallen; they did not cut it down, not having tools fitted for that, nor had they the means to transport it; they had them ready-made in nearly all the places to which they went.

For making them, they employed stone axes, well-sharpened, and set into the end of a forked stick [where they were] well tied. With these axes they cut a little into the top of the wood at the length they wished the kettle. This done they placed fire on top and made the tree burn. When burnt about four inches in depth they removed the fire, and then with stones and huge pointed bones, as large as the thumb, they hollowed it out the best they could, removing all the burnt part. Then they replaced the fire, and when it was again burnt they removed it all from the interior and commenced again to separate the burnt part, continuing this until their kettle was big enough for their fancy, and that was oftener too big than too little.

Here, finally, is the primary cooking vessel that is naturally missing from the archaeological record. Denys went on to describe in detail how fire-reddened stones were used to bring the water to boil. Almost as an afterthought, he added, "they had always a supply of soup, which was their greatest drink." Turning to Le Clercq, we find acknowledgement, in his *Nouvelle Relation de la Gaspesie* that

> many find it difficult to understand the manner in which the Indians boiled their meat before they were given the use of our kettles, which they now find extremely convenient. I have learned from themselves that before they obtained our kettles, they used little buckets or troughs of wood, which they filled with water; into this they threw glowing stones....

It is highly significant that the three principal sources on the seventeenth-century Mi'kmaq all described these stationary, tree-trunk cauldrons. Two of them, Denys and Le Clercq, took some pains to make it clear that these were utilized in olden times, before the advent of the copper kettle, and in light of this clarification it is conjectured that Marc Lescarbot was spectator to an essentially aboriginal piece of handiwork. Moreover, Lescarbot's account has special meaning, since it is likewise a commentary on technological obsolescence. The adze which, in stark contrast with other coastal Algonkian sites, is so common in the artifactual remains of prehistoric Mi'kmaq settlements, was apparently replaced by the iron hatchet as the preferred tool for hollowing out trunk kettles. Presumably, incidents such as this one of improvised kettle construction must have become increasingly rare after the copper kettle entered the mainstream of Mi'kmaw domestic life.

If we are to trust Denys, and there is no reason not to, the new copper kettle conferred upon the Mi'kmaq an unprecedented degree of mobility. "The axes, the kettles, the knives, and everything that is supplied them," he unhesitatingly declared,

is much more convenient and portable than those which they had in former times, when they were obliged to go to camp near their grotesque kettles, in place of which to-day they are free to go camp where they wish. One can say that in those times the immovable kettles were the chief regulators of their lives, since they were able to live only in places where these were.

And again:

They have good axes, knives more convenient for their work, and kettles easy to carry. This is a great convenience for them, as they are not obliged to go to the places where were their kettles of wood, of which one never sees any at present, as they have entirely abandoned the use of them.

We might interject that Denys is considered a highly reliable source on Mi'kmaq customs. As George MacBeath, his biographer in the *Dictionary of Canadian Biography: 1000 to 1700*, phrased it, he was a man possessed of a "thorough knowledge of his subject."

Fitting all of the above pieces of evidence together, it is clear that the early historic Mi'kmaq had a seasonal migration pattern of winters spent inland and summers spent on the coast. There is, furthermore, compelling evidence that this practice may have been aboriginal, although one cannot be certain. From Nicolas Denys we are led to believe that Mi'kmaq households habitually repaired to interior or coastal campsites where were located their stationary, tree-trunk cauldrons. Of course it would be naive to suggest that the location of Mi'kmaw settlement was determined by the position of these wooden cauldrons. Quite the reverse, Mi'kmaq households picked an area for its potential resources and other delights, and then fashioned a cauldron as a matter of course.

We know from early French accounts of this settlement process that interior campsites were invariably either riverine, lacustrine, or (we may add) tidal pond in their orientation. Coastal sites were probably most commonly situated in bays, again along a river- or stream-bank. Evidently this procedure applied to both individual families and, in a loose sense, to groups of families, or bands—bands typically derived their name from a prominent river, and band chiefs were said to preside over a certain river district. Thus, in sum, individual households were accustomed to locate a campsite beside a body of water which was in the vicinity of the band river. And there they hewed out their ungainly wooden cauldrons. In keeping with the dictates of the seasons, families moved from seacost to interior and back again, invariably setting up camp in the shadow of their wooden cauldrons—vessels which eventually acquired a mildly magnetic quality, in the sense that they came to symbolize the domestic focus of the clamming beach or hunting area. This must be what Denys had in mind when he referred to the regulatory effect these had on Mi'kmaq seasonal migration and settlement habits.

Then came the fur trade, and with it an overpowering urge to range indiscriminately, to hunt beyond the usual bounds of one's area in search of the precious pelts and hides. As the prices of these articles soared, furbearers and browsers were hounded to near extinction—an ecological and (for the Indian) cultural catastrophe facilitated by the portable copper kettle. Recalling Denys' words, the kettle conferred upon these people the freedom "to go camp where they wish." The implication is that in a logistic sense, the copper kettle shares in the responsibility for the reckless slaughter of wildlife attendant upon the seventeenth-century Acadian fur trade. The wooden cauldrons were now rendered obsolete, both practically and symbolically. For, where they had stood for permanence and stability, their successor the copper kettle bespoke mobility and chaos.

We judge there was chaos from the curious fact that the Mi'kmaq resorted to an allotment system of land tenure in the late seventeenth century. "It is the right of the head of the nation," revealed Le Clercq, "according to the customs of the country, which serve as laws and regulations to the Gaspesians (Mi'kmaq), to distribute the places of hunting to each individual. It is not permitted to any Indian to overstep the bounds and limits of the region which shall have been assigned him in the assemblies of the elders. These are held in autumn and spring expressly to make this assignment." No doubt, by "the head of the nation" Le Clercq was referring to the headman of the individual bands, as he makes clear in another passage. "The occupation of this chief [from the Restigouche River] was to assign the places for hunting, and to take the furs of the Indians, giving them in turn whatever they needed."

Very likely there was some precedent for the allotment system in the re-allocation prerogatives of the headmen. Biard, writing three-quarters of a century before Le Clercq, recalled that the sagamore, as he called the headman, was the eldest son of a powerful family. "All the young people of the family are at his table and in his retinue; it is also his duty to provide dogs for the chase, canoes for transportation, provisions and reserves for bad weather and expeditions. The young people flatter him, hunt, and serve their apprenticeship under him, not being allowed to have anything before they are married." The sagamore was reportedly entitled to all the game taken by these youthful apprentices, but only a portion of the catch of a married man. When one of the latter returned from either a hunting expedition or with other supplies, he would scrupulously pay his "dues and homage in skins and like gifts." To be headman was a coveted office, and Biard makes it clear that there was plenty of intrigue for it. Considering, therefore, the commercial incentives associated with the unrestrained character of fur hunting and trapping in the early years of the seventeenth century, it is not difficult to imagine how the headman's function in re-allocating community resources was extended to embrace the allotment of community lands toward the close of the century.

The copper kettle, in a word, by virtue of its portable, sturdy nature, made it easier for these people to roam the woods in search of furbearers—easier than it would have been had they been obliged to rely on the stationary wooden cauldrons. Granted, they could have hacked out temporary cauldrons as they moved about the bush, reminiscent of Lescarbot's experience, but that is not the point. The Mi'kmaq would have responded to the lure of the fur trade the way they did with or without the copper kettle; the point is that the kettle facilitated (intensified) their mobility. Although it is only conjectural, the evidence of mass slaughter of wildlife, Denys' cryptic allusions to nomadism, and the belated imposition of an allotment system to safeguard territorial boundaries—all seem to suggest that the copper kettle was one element in a complex of forces which overthrew the traditional settlement pattern and mode of land tenure (obscure as it is). One can take this kind of argument too far, of course, to where it begins to sound like technological determinism. That is emphatically not our intention here, however. Kettles, like many other forms of technology, are capable of being put to many uses and defined in just as many ways. In this sense they follow—they offer possibilities—rather than lead.

Reminiscent of Pierre Biard, with whom we began, we concede that trade goods lists are undoubtedly tedious records of culture contact, that is, they are if one does not interrogate them for their deeper mysteries. Examples such as this show the implications which at least some of these items posed for the native recipients. The picture that emerges is one of the assimilation into the native economic, ceremonial, spiritual, and demographic context, in the case of the kettle, anyway. Presumably other trade goods fulfilled other functions and acquired other definitions as each was incorporated into an existing, on-going scheme of things. European hardware was what the Indian thought it was and was made to serve the purposes to which he put it. Each thus assumed a new personality—a native identity quite different, perhaps, from its manufacturer's intended identity. So it was that an iron-handled, twenty five by thirteen-inch copper kettle was culturally transformed from a secular object of commerce (in the donor society), into an animated commercial-ceremonial institution offering unprecedented demographic possibilities to the receptor society. Which is an academic way of saying that copper kettles can be more than simply convenient cooking vessels, as the French chroniclers of the seventeenth-century Mi'kmaq so vividly testified.

This essay is edited from Calvin Martin's original article in *Ethnohistory,* Number 22, 1975. Formerly a professor of history at Rutgers University, he has published several books, including *Keepers of the Game: Indian-Animal Relationships and the Fur Trade* and *The Way of the Human Being*.

Ebenezer McMillan, an 1856 pioneer who followed Rev. Norman McLeod from St. Ann's, Cape Breton, to Waipu, New Zealand, at the monument to the six ships and their passengers, in Waipu.

10

My Quest for Rev. Norman McLeod

Flora McPherson

FLORA McPHERSON'S *Watchman Against the World: The Remarkable Journey of Norman McLeod & his People from Scotland to Cape Breton Island to New Zealand* undoubtedly ranks as a Cape Breton Classic. But Flora MacPherson grew up in Ontario, not Cape Breton. And we wanted to know how she came to research and write *Watchman*. During a phone conversation, she said that the book grew out of a 1946 bike trip to Cape Breton. Then, a few days later, we got a letter from Flora.

FLORA McPHERSON: I'm sorry that I gave the off-the-cuff response that *Watchman* was written because of a holiday bike trip in 1946—a flippant answer to a sudden question. That was my first sight of Cape Breton but the book actually happened because it fitted into a pattern developed long before.

My older relatives had lived in widely scattered parts of Canada. They were eager storytellers, fond of recalling the past. They were not celebrities and did not brag of their own achievements, but they took active parts in their community life. When they came to visit in Ontario they chatted about what they had experienced or about the background of their communities.

Like many only children, I often listened to adult conversations. Life in other times and places in Canada was very interesting to me because of its connection with these talkative visitors. I couldn't understand why most of my friends found Canadian history deadly dull.

I presently realized that for the bored people it was made up of a series of remote celebrities—politicians, explorers and other "great men" formally presented in thick, sombre volumes—while for me it was peopled by groups of individuals making a living in communities as we did, but affected by strong or unusual people who came among them.

I thought that these latter stories could attract a wider audience to Canadian history and help to display its range and variety. They would need to be carefully researched and presented on an adult level, not as sociological studies of communities, but as biographies of persons who influenced their community or their country. The books should not be tediously long—perhaps about 200 pages. Presumably they should have the immediacy of local history but would be supported by research into the background.

This idea stayed dormant for many years; I kept testing it by examining source material on individuals who seemed interesting. I finally struck something intriguing when Mary Barber and I were collecting material for a book called *Christmas in Canada*. We found a few paragraphs about some Scottish people in Cape Breton who, in the 1850s, built six sailing ships and transplanted themselves to New Zealand under the leadership of a strong, autocratic minister, Norman McLeod. The story was new to us both. Not long afterward we found a newly published book by a New Zealand writer—Neil Robinson's *Lion of Scotland*—telling the story from the New Zealand point of view and skimming very lightly over the Canadian part.

We thought of the migration story as an adventure book for Canadian young people, and considered collaborating on it. Lack of free time made this impossible, but as a critic and a sounding board for my ideas, Mary was completely involved from beginning to end.

During my holidays in 1954 I spent a week in the Public Archives of Nova Scotia searching for material on St. Ann's, Cape Breton, which was the Canadian home of Norman McLeod and his migrant community. Then on to the village of Baddeck in Cape Breton where the librarian sent me to Mrs. Kathryn Mackenzie, a descendant of a member of the St. Ann's community. She had a copy of *The Gael Fares Forth*, another New Zealand book long out of print.

With a proper appreciation of such a book's value, Mrs. Mackenzie would not let it out of her house, so I settled down in her living room and, as she fed me cookies and tea, I scribbled pages of notes. What was most exciting was that a part of the book was based on letters written by Murdoch Macdonald, Mrs. Mackenzie's grand-uncle, who had come to St. Ann's with the first settlers in 1820, as a twelve-year-old boy, and lived in the settlement throughout the thirty years before the migration to New Zealand. I wanted more than anything to get my hands on those letters. They were thought to be in the basement of the county court house at Baddeck, somewhere among the accumulation of 50 years' unfiled, unindexed material. They may be there yet, as I never found them. The very fact that such things could disappear made me all the more anxious to collect and keep all the scattered scraps that would make the story.

When I left London, Ontario, in 1955 to work in the Galt Public Library, I took my folder of notes with me but they were never once unpacked in Galt. However, for a year and a half in Galt I wrote a weekly column on library-related subjects in the

113

local paper. For this I owe more to the Galt Library than to any library whose help I have acknowledged in the foreward to the book—without the experience of regular writing I would not have been ready to write a book and would not have had sufficient confidence to begin it.

Presently I felt that I must try it, and that the only way was to give up my job and write. So for a year I lived on half my salary and saved the other half. My salary that year was $4100, but excellent five-pound cheeses were cheap at Baden and it was easy to buy bushels of luscious red apples at St. George.

In the summer of 1958 I moved to part of a farmhouse at Arva to live on the other half of the salary, in a place which ideally combined country life and accessible libraries. Since I knew that Norman McLeod had spent the year 1826 in Caledonia, New York, I went that fall to see the village and search through the well-indexed records in its old stone library; then on to Washington to visit friends and spend a week using the Library of Congress, searching for material on church and community life in New York state in the 1820s. I came back with many notes which are the basis of two pages in the published book. I have been told by an authority on non-fiction writing that, in a history or biography, the final book consists of about 2% of the accumulated material. You don't ignore the other 98%—you try to assimilate it and build your impressions from it.

I also had to know very thoroughly the Scottish county where Norman McLeod lived from 1780 to 1812 before he came to North America, and every possible detail of community life there. The University library had an excellent collection on this subject; so good that when I visited Sutherlandshire, Scotland, in 1960 after I had finished the book, I felt completely at home in the countryside which I had been describing.

I was faring rather well in background material, but at the beginning of 1959 one vital primary source was still evading me—the one book written by McLeod himself. It was a tremendous satisfaction finally to discover a copy in the Legislative Library in Halifax and get the tattered volume at Western on interlibrary loan—for use only in the library, of course. The book—*The Pres-*

ent Church of Scotland and a Tint of Normanism Contending in a Dialogue — was a strange combination of personal reminiscences, sermons and theological diatribes. I knew that I must keep from it every phrase and idea that might even possibly be useful, so I copied frantically in all my spare time for three weeks (I was now back working half-time at the London Library). I sorted, indexed and cross-indexed as I went. For the next month I couldn't read at all. Copying from tiny closely-spaced print and old yellowed pages is one of the hazards of history-writing.

At last I was ready to begin writing. I had decided that it couldn't be a teen-age adventure story. The motives of the characters were too complex to be ignored or to be explained simply. It had to be a biography for adults. For my own satisfaction, I wanted it to be not just the story of a man who was a dictator, but also a study of leadership and of the narrow line in a person's thought and conduct between a sense of public responsibility and active dictatorship. That seemed a universal and timeless problem.

Gradually, a chapter a week, regularly scrutinized and appraised by Mary Barber, it began to take shape. Writing revealed many more things that I wanted to know — what colour were the students' gowns in King's College, Aberdeen, in 1812? What wild flowers might be in bloom in Cape Breton late in May? What would Pictou harbour look like as one sailed into it in the early fall of 1817? (Since I was a librarian I did the research myself; I didn't phone the reference room.) By the summer I was discouraged; I still did not know enough about the McLeod family and the inner working of the community. I took a month off and went again to Nova Scotia, driving this time, and taking my mother along for a holiday. In the Archives in Halifax I found much newly-processed material not available on my first visit.

There was one major unanswered question: Why, when the settlers at St. Ann's were starving because of crop failures, did they not get help from John Munro, a powerful entrepreneur, whose shipping and lumbering business employed many people of the settlement? I puzzled over it for months. Finally, on my last days in the Archives, I was shown a microfilm of the few remaining pre-1851 issues of the newspaper, *The Cape Breton Spectator*. In one was a letter to the editor from John Munro, explaining how and why, in their great need, Norman had made his people boycott Munro's business. That was the most vivid moment in the writing of the book. I was too shy to shriek with delight in the scholarly silence of the Archives. I wrote "This is it!" in a huge black scrawl, across my page, and I'm sure I grinned ear to ear.

Not publication, but moments like this, are the thrill of doing a book.

Presently I had typed the completed manuscript in the prescribed form and it went off in June 1960 to look for a publisher....

I was appalled to hear from the publishers that they wanted ten illustrations—for a book set in the period 1800-1860! Of course, some of them could be landscape, present-day. A Cape Breton librarian spent a day taking pictures for me at St. Ann's; a family I had met in Lochinver, Scotland, found photographs of the landscape for me, and the clerk of Assynt parish in Scotland provided an excellent photograph along with a letter on the unworthiness of Norman as the subject of a book!

Here is my reply to that clerk:

I could not completely squelch my interest in Norman McLeod for two reasons. The first is that I am particularly interested in leadership—in the qualities that create leaders and followers anywhere and in any time. I wanted to assess what established his leadership, what maintained his power even over people who were wiser in mind and greater in spirit than he. This is important to me because I think that civilized people must know not only when they are being led but why they are being led and what they are giving up for the security of having leadership. In writing of him I was constantly aware of parallels, both small and great, in the present-day world. I mention it to you only to explain my belief that a study of a small-scale tyrant is not untimely or unnecessary.

My second reason is that I am a Canadian, interested in the social history of our country and in the small settlements from which it grew. The story of the Canadian years of McLeod and his people is therefore important, whatever McLeod's character may have been. Indeed, much as we Canadians might like to idealize our founders, we find in many of them a streak of ruthlessness which is not likeable, but may well have been the only force which could weld and sustain an immigrant people in the lonely vastness of this country. The confidence of many leaders must have had to be dangerously near to self-deification to supply the strength which weaker members needed. To us McLeod is particularly obnoxious because of his all-pervading power which we must be sure that many of the people under him hated and resented. But I also know that Colonel Thomas Talbot, under whom the part of Ontario where I live was settled, was stoutly hated by some of his settlers. His power was by no means religious, but it was wielded in many ways and his  aims for his settlement were not particularly altruistic. Yet without such hard men Canada might not exist. Certainly many of the weaker spirits would not have pulled through without their strength.

You will notice, however, that their people, protected by their leaders' strength at first, eventually grew around and beyond them.

MY OLD FRIENDS at the Nova Scotia Archives cooperated once more and the New Brunswick Museum produced a drawing of Norman. The most remarkable help came from the Alexander Turnbull Library in Wellington, New Zealand, whose staff searched relentlessly for the material I wanted and produced a good selection of drawings of the ships and some photographs. By February 1962 the illustrations were on their way (to the publisher). The file of correspondence about them is 2 1/2 inches thick!

People are frequently saying that they would or could write a book, but they haven't time. That's not strictly true. Anyone has time to write, even while he is working for a living, provided that he gives up all his social life, loses contact with most of his friends, joins no organizations, and makes his family take second place to his writing—in other words, if he is willing to gamble that the contribution he might make to his community and to his own satisfaction, by writing, is great enough to compensate for all these deprivations. It's a long shot and it probably won't come off. What you need in order to try it is not just lots of time, but lots of nerve, and a few friends who keep rooting for you, even for eight years!

11

Architect at the Fortress of Louisbourg

Yvon LeBlanc

A FTER 12 YEARS HERE, I'm still enthused by the view of the thing. Every morning when I come to work, seeing it under different light, it's still quite taking. You know, when there's fog, when you just see it through — beautiful sunlight and all that — oh, it's a dilly. And I was lucky. I came here for the last part of my career. Because for other people, younger ones, coming here with a young family, needing social life and all that — oh, it's awfully hard. (*To live in Louisbourg?*) Oh, yes. It is out of the way. And especially French-speaking ones. That is why we never

could get French-speaking people here, as much as we would have needed. Because it is a fringe region to people from inland.

(*Would people from the eighteenth century, living here, have felt as cut off?*) Oh, they must have. The few comments we have are usually bad. They were cut off, far away. Although they had quite a lot going on here, you know—dances and gambling and dinners and things like that. Especially during carnival time, which was from the beginning of the year up to Lent. They had lots of dances and balls and dinners and meetings—especially in the second occupation (1749-1758). In the first one (1713-1745), we don't have as much information on those activities. We wish we had more—letters, more personal things.

We know that they had certain celebrations. The Feast of St. Louis, for instance, 25th of August. In the first period there's a description of a celebration they had on the occasion when the king, who had been sick, got well. And there was some celebration at the birth of the dauphin, the king's first son. Because King Louis got several girls all in a row. Then finally, he got a son in 1729, and that was the future king. So they had some celebrations. (*And your studies for the architecture of Louisbourg, they include even this?*) It's the people. That's the part which was interesting to me here: working for people, trying to imagine people who have been dead for 250 years. In other words, building for clients who have long been dead. In order to try to make up my mind about how their house was.

ONE OF OUR LATEST BUILDINGS is called the de la Plagne house. He was the nephew of one of the officers here, de Pensens, who owned this land. And maybe it was his uncle who built it, we're not sure. We found the foundations. Very soon after it was built, there was a lawsuit. A soldier came and stole something from it, and he went in front of the court. It's a very sad kind of story. Most of our stories are rather sad. This one was a young soldier who was on guard one night, not long after the house had been built. And he came out for—as he calls it—his necessities. And he was right at the corner of that fence we see here today. There was a latrine there, we think; we're not absolutely sure it was still there at that time. Anyway, he was there, doing his thing, and he saw this house; and he remembered that he had worked here earlier as a servant, and he knew they were

The de la Plagne house

fairly rich. This all comes out at the interrogation.

He climbs over the gate on the other side, comes inside, lifts one of the window panes, puts his hand inside, unhooks and goes in. And he steals some money and a pair of white gloves. The next morning, the Negro slave, the servant in this house, came down and saw the pane hanging out. That's how the theft was found out. And he was reported and he was caught. He was in a tavern. He wasn't a very bright fellow. I think he was a very young man, an orphan, about 20 years old.

Then, of course, the outcome of the story is very sad. There's a first account. And then there was another account of it, which says this: that after he went through the first trial, he was sentenced, and some people thought the sentence was not hard enough—so the whole thing started again. All through the whole interrogation and everything. And in the course of one of the interrogations, a very touching scene happened. The judge was making a review of the information, of the testimonies, and he interrogated Mrs. de la Plagne. And he asked her if she had anything to add to her testimony of before. She said something like, "Yes. On a certain date, I was in front of my house, and a young soldier went by with guards. He broke away. He came and threw himself on his knees in front of me, and said he would never do it again—asking me to pardon him." And then, that second time, he was hanged. So, we have the whole series of questions and answers. We could put that on the stage as it is and make a beautiful play out of it. A touching story.

As far as the building itself, the de la Plagne house, we had, when it was sold, mention of this: it was boarded inside and out. It was a wood frame building, garnished, as they call it, with stone and brick. In other words, stone and brick between the frame, inside the wall. We presume it's that. That's all we can do. Then boarded inside and out. That is why, on the inside, where we see one of the walls, we filled the bottom part with stone and the upper part with brick—presuming when they said with stone and brick, maybe they went one floor stone and the other floor brick. And then we sort of deduced things from that, assuming that that was it.

For instance, in the archeological work, we had found in the foundation some traces of the wood plate on top of the foundation—not very very strong, but some trace. It seemed to be about 12 inches thick, 12 *pouces*—which was the old French—a *pouce* is about 1/16th more than our inch. So from that, we deduced that probably the ground floor framework of the wall was 12 *pouces* by 12 *pouces*, as we knew some others were, by documentation. And that's a good thickness for stone. And at the upper part—it often happened that the upper floors of buildings were thinner, making that, say, 8 inches or so—and so we filled that with brick. So it's a lot of detective work, really.

We also know that the glass of the window panes was held in with points, and then on the outside there were strips of blue paper. In the 1720s, there's an account in France, saying there's this new thing, this putty, that you put on the outside of the window—it stops the drafts from coming in. But they say that now, since that hardens very soon, you can't take the panes off to clean them. In other words, when they had paper around them, they took each pane out to clean them. Now we know that here at Louisbourg they had strips of paper also. Because this fellow, when he went into the house, he lifted one of the panes, he put his arm in. And the next morning, the slave saw the pane hanging out. Therefore, this house, built in about 1740, had the paper holding the glass in. But we put putty today, because we have to. We haven't found a proper paper and glue which would answer to some extent our present need for maintenance. So for the moment—and since we do know that they were starting to use putty here occasionally—we've taken the liberty for the moment to use some putty. Though some fine day, you may find little strips of glued paper.

(*But you really want to be that precise?*) Oh, we're trying to be as precise as we can. We have to do things for modern needs, but we go out of our way to do it as close as possible as it was. Now, quite often we're not absolutely sure. As close as possible as we have reason to think it was. If we have to do something else, for some reason, we like to have it written down that we did it, but knowingly. Sometimes we have to guess. And that is why, when I first came here, my whole point was to try to sort of imbibe myself of everything I could find out about building anything of that time, so that when the time for guessing comes, well, I guess with that influencing my guess. That's the best we can do.

The boarding of the de la Plagne house—that's purely invention, but justified by this: the gate down at the bottom of the street, the Frederic Gate, is built in wood—we have a drawing of it. And it shows strips of wood, with the deep joint. These both were built about the same time. We know this house was planked, or boarded. And since we knew that they were fairly well-to-do—on and on like that—we figured that, well, this house could very well have been boarded like the Frederic Gate. But we have no real firsthand reason to think that.

Now, we're still mystified about what we're going to do with the stone part of the de la Plagne house. Because the foundations that were found are very, very clear, that this part was obviously an addition. We had to presume that it was there in 1745; we're not absolutely sure. We have a drawing—a general view of the town, seen from outside—where we see this building, what we think is this building. And this end here, the extended part of the building, is not very clear. So, oh, we hemmed and hawed a long time before building that part. There's a later drawing, 1758. It's a strangely interesting drawing; it's a sort of a bird's-eye view of the town, based on imagination, largely. And it's all sort of distorted. But it's amazing how you can recognize some of the buildings. And this building, we see it. We see the number of windows. But we don't see any difference in the wall surface. It was very, very small scale, you know, and it's a thing which the artist might not have noticed. But on the other hand, it could have meant that either the planking continued over the stone extension, or that the same paint would have been applied on the stone surface. The stones could have been given a coat of mortar, and then the whole thing painted the same colour as the boards. And that's what we may do, eventually. We don't know yet. For the moment, it's raw stone, and we're still deliberating. Oh, there's lots of little decisions to take yet.

That is why now, since I'm leaving this summer, I'm preparing a summary of all the buildings. I have to include a comment on each building, saying the things that now, by hindsight, we could have done differently.

We worked in a team, a design team. There's a historian, an archeologist, a draftsman, and the architect, who's chairman of the team. And we gather all the information from those different aspects. And then we put all that together, see what we can deduce. And then I fill the holes by going into architectural background, how people lived at that time, secondary historical documents, archeology—what different pieces might mean. It's a question of putting things together. And then, from what we know of the individuals themselves. Now me, as an architect, I've always been people-oriented in architecture. So, I went as far as I could to get as much as I could about feeling about the people themselves.

THE DE GANNES HOUSE was one of the earlier buildings I worked on. And I don't think I worked in enough of that. I had not imbibed enough of the people at that very early stage. That is why, now, I'm going to recommend that we change the interior batten doors, to put doors which have a bit better finish. In a house like this, the doors probably were what we call the *emboîture* doors, that is, the doors which are flush. All sorts of little things haven't been solved yet. Or things that I'm getting solved now, after years. It takes a long time. As a matter of fact, it was only after about four years here, that I began to feel a little bit comfortable about guessing, that I could trust my imagination, that it would be sufficiently coloured by all that I had imbibed.

De Gannes was a captain of one of the companies here. He

Architect at the Fortress of Louisbourg

was born at Port Royal in Acadia, to a military family. But he's not an Acadian, as such. He was born there—but to us Acadians, there's a difference. He was born there; his father was in the military there;

The de Gannes house

but he was not a settler, he was not an Acadian, not as the people who had settled down there. If you lived in England, even if you were born there, it makes you an English citizen as such—but it doesn't make you an Englishman.

(*I had heard that de Gannes was wealthy enough to build a house like de la Plagne. But because he was from Acadia, not France, and had experienced Maritime winters, he chose a smaller, more humble house—but one easier to heat.*) That's interesting. That comes from me. Because, as an Acadian, I'm trying like mad to find out what the Acadian houses were like. We have extremely little on Acadian houses. Now there is this: he was born in Acadia, but we don't know too much about his youth, whether he actually lived there. Because, at that late period—this house was built in the 1740s—he built with *piquet*. The *piquet* type building—that is, with the vertical logs in the ground—was a type of building which was built at the very first in Louisbourg, as a very quick way of building, a nearly temporary way of building. That's my opinion. Because, it's a very inefficient way of building, logs in the ground. Although we are amazed how some of them lasted; one built in 1713 was still there in 1745. Still, it's quite astonishing that he, an officer, 30 years after the start, still built in that technique.

And we found the foundation, and we found the traces of the *piquets* in the ground. It's on account of his building here that way, that we wonder whether the Acadians did not build like that

125

in Port Royal as well. We don't know how they built in Port Royal. In some of our other buildings, you'll see the *piquet* technique exposed. Here, during the archeological excavation, we found little bits of plaster in the foundation, so we presume that the interior was plastered, or partly. We don't really know. We tried both. We covered some with boards, and some with the plaster. And you'll notice we arranged the plaster to show slightly the form of the *piquet* underneath. But by far, the interiors seemed much, much more often boarded than plastered inside.

Building this modest little house in 1742, de Gannes must have gone through a very low time, a difficult time business-wise. Because he had owned three lots in town, on which one had a house from quite early, where he must have lived. He died in '52. And we know that in the early '40s, when he sold his lots, he was living on another of his lots. So therefore he had two houses. We know he sold those three lots in a fairly short period of time. We know he'd sold all his lots, so it's by that that we presume that he was living here. This house shows on the first English plan in 1745. So it's by all that surmising that we figure he was here. What we really only know is that he died here. Because, when he died, it's definitely this house, by the inventory.

But why would he build such a house? His wife was from an engineer's family, de Catalogne. She died in 1750. Around that time, his daughter got married. She got a dowry of over 10,000 *livres*, of which he had paid 8,000 at his death. Therefore, he must have been quite well off. Oh yes, and when the family came back after the first siege, three of his daughters came back with him. They had interesting names. Whereas, usually you're Mary or Anne or something like that, they were Mademoiselle de la—Something or Other—Mademoiselle de So-and-So. That seems to mean that they had become attached to some property in France. They came with four servants. And they presumably settled down in this house. Three girls and a son, the father and mother, four servants who might have been living there. So therefore, they must have been fairly well off. But it's not a house which seems to indicate that kind of living. (*Because of the use of* piquet?) And small, and sort of temporary. The modesty of the building does not seem to add up. Whether it was a choice... or influence, or perhaps he built it when he was in low means in the '40s. We just don't know. When he died, he had lots of stuff, but there were lots of old things. And it appeared that his family was not living with him—there was no evidence of the family in his inventory. Although often they didn't inventory the things considered belonging to the children or others. So that is why it makes it difficult for us at times.

But to come back to the house. The Acadian thing—that is partly me trying to explain why he did that. And maybe this *is* some little indication of how some houses at Port Royal might have been. It's very thin, our thing. And I'd like to find out. Now, when the archeological sources tell us, "a fireplace, centrally located in the house"—that can really be two fireplaces. It is a normal thing to do in a small house, because you can heat two rooms with one mass. Now, I've heard it said how the engineer was stupid building his great big house, whereas this guy, de Gannes, up the hill there, he was much brighter—he built a small house around a fireplace. That is the kind of myth we have to debunk, because we just don't know. It goes without saying that a house like this was more comfortable. Is that why de Gannes built it? Intentionally and all that? But that's another story.

Now look at the roof—this was re-roofed recently. That's one of our maintenance problems; things that don't last very long here. This had to be re-roofed after only 6 or 7 years. That's a problem with the climate. I would like to paint some of the roofs. (*Does anything stop you?*) Oh yes, yes, yes. See, we always hold our heads, and everything has to be thought out and justified with great care. And I would like to paint some of them because there is some mention of paint in our papers. None connected with roofs, except there have been pieces of shingles found with traces of colour on them. But any mention of paint is just as often to complain that there was not enough of it. There were some paint shipments arriving, there's some yellow ochre and quite a lot of red ochre. But we know there was a lack of paint. So we are still hemming and hawing and discussing all that, because we have to reflect. We want to be very serious.

The Duhaget house

FOR THE DUHAGET HOUSE, we have no inventory, no nothing on that. We think there was some paint on it; there might have been some paint applied. That is, in one of the rental agreements, there is some hint — but we're not sure, we're not sure. And we'd like to paint it, because our houses are deteriorating with the weather and all that — the exposed wood. Oh, it's a big worry we have. And we'd like to paint them all. If we could get evidence. Although we have no definite evidence one way or the other, there are certainly indications that a lot were not painted. There's no doubt about that. So that is why we're a bit leery.

(*The Duhaget is one for which you've not made decisions on the interior.*) That's right. It's a bit bigger than others. We knew it had two floors. We knew that Duhaget was captain of a company. We have reason to believe that he may have been not too badly off. We also tend to believe that he built that rather big house, planning to have a family, but he didn't have any. And then, there was a later view of it which showed it fairly high. Therefore, it was quite a substantial house. We had a terrific controversy about the roof. When I arrived, they were just starting to work on it, whether it should be the gable roof or the hip roof. Some of the views were contradictory. Working by team, you see, and working by a sort of majority vote — it was not easy for an architect.

The placing of board: vertical on the upper part, horizontal on the lower part. We knew this house was framed — we found traces of the posts and all that. And therefore I think we presumed it was boarded, or maybe we had some reason to believe it was boarded. Now, as it was high, and a sense of the place, that it was a fairly large house, boards all the same width could have been very dull. Since we do see buildings with a different kind of finish on the ground floor part and on the upper part—well, using wood both places, the only possible way to vary it was one horizontal and one vertical. So that's really how we came to that. It's purely to give it a bit of a shape, of a look, on account of the size. That's the only reason we did that. And it's quite plausible.

Most of the houses that I worked with, what we find—the foundation and the location of the fireplace—usually gives us a pretty good idea of how it was divided inside. But this one has me stumped. The way the fireplace is—I haven't found an interior distribution of rooms which makes any sense. So it's got me stumped. It's the only one, really.

BUT WHEN THERE'S SOMETHING DEFINITE, we of course try to stick to that. For the Lartigue house, for instance, we have a document which is dated 1753—probably done after that—when Widow Lartigue was showing the state of her estate, the houses she owned, pieces of land here and there. So we followed this, but with great, great care. There are so many errors, we had to make up our mind on a lot of things. There's a note on it saying how the pieces of frame were 12 by 12 *pouces* pine wood, filled with rough stone between the posts— put on a foundation of stone, about one *pied* and a half above the street. [One *pied* is 1.066 feet.] So we could observe that very well.

There are little mysteries again. Here we found the foundation. What was found did not completely reflect the drawing. For instance, there was very clear

The Lartigue house

evidence of the floorboards and joists and things. But they were found below the top of the foundation wall. That would mean that you would have gone up two steps, and then gone down. That doesn't add up. We never figured that one out. Also, there was some paving in the house, at the back, some stone and brick paving at two spots, which were down at the level of the floor. We know that this building was used much later by the English as a stable or something else like that. And for the moment, we attributed those things to that second occupation, and had to leave the mystery. The mystery is still there. We're building for 1744, and all we can surmise is that the floor was at the level of the bottom of the door. That's the way we built it. But we haven't really solved the mysteries yet.

The Lartigue house is interesting, because there were quite a lot of people living in there. And at first glance, they could have been quite squeezed in. But it worked out that they could have had about 18 people in that, without being all that overcrowded. The way it was laid out. (*Do you mean, the way you chose to lay it out?*) No, the way I found out that it probably was, by following the indications. I chose because I was being led—that there were the two fireplace bases, and all that. And also, led by a typical way that houses were at that time: houses of a certain size, where the rooms were in groups, in suites. You find that in elaborate townhouses, great big houses. Even in this rather small one, as far as townhouses go, you could have a group of three rooms on one side of the stair. And on the other side of the stair, you could have a group of three rooms. And often the rooms go one into the other.

We had enough room to make a hallway; and they often had that. Because the sense of privacy at that time was a bit different from ours, since beds had curtains around—a room was a room, not necessarily a bedroom. A living room could easily have a bed in it. Or a bedroom could also be for living in, on account of the curtains. So, people travelling through a room was not that unheard of. And in this house, it would reflect that quite easily. Although, we knew something about the house: we found the foundation and we had the elevation [a drawing of the face of the house]. That's all we had. And the date that he died. And the number of his family, including a daughter who had married. As part of the dowry or wedding arrangement, we knew Lartigue was going to lodge them for a period of time. And with them in there, with a couple of children—I think there were some servants—they could have fitted there quite easily, not more than two per room. Some of the rooms were smallish. And still leaving a big general area where they could have dined, where the stair came down—leaving a largish room for him to conduct his business as a judge.

(*Do you ever have these people come to you in any way?*) I dearly wish that they would! Oh, I dream of that! It's not that I dream of them as such—no, I haven't dreamt of them. But I find myself speaking in the present sometimes, of that time. People have a good laugh at me, that I speak of them as present, or speak of "us."

For instance, about the Royal Battery out there. It's a very sad story about that, how it never was used. Because at the first siege, they were in the process of doing some repairs on it, and they felt they could not defend it. It had some weaknesses; there were some hills around. But it had been made to shoot at the entrance to the harbour, to protect the harbour. So anyway, they decided to abandon it, when the English were coming. (*Because they came by land.*) Yes. That is a very sore point to me, because the engineer, Verrier [here from 1724 to 1745], he's really my predecessor here.

When they decided that they could not defend the Royal Battery, and decided to give it up, they discussed the possibility of blowing it up completely. It was Verrier, the engineer, who was instrumental in stopping that decision, making the decision that they should spike the cannon to stop them from being fired. And then withdraw all the ammunition. Now, that was decided. Some people have looked very crossly at Verrier for doing that, that he did that because he was very proud of his Royal Battery, he didn't want to see it destroyed. Well, I think that's not so at all. I think he was hoping that it could be protected, and that they could get it back after and still use it. But they got panic-stricken, and they didn't properly spike the cannon. So that a couple of days after, the English were shooting at us with our own cannon and balls. And look, I find myself saying, "They were shooting at us." Which makes people laugh.

We've all got our own people that we prefer or like, that we get more involved with. And Verrier, he was a sort of dullish kind of person. But he's accused of all sorts of things, and I feel bound to try to put things straight. They accuse him of wasting money on building the big gates, monumental gates. They say, if he had been working at his fortification rather than at that, it might have been better. But what I tried to make them realize, it ain't necessarily so. Because at that time, in the times of kings, the monumental entrances to a town were extremely important. They express the prestige of the king. And in architecture and in the mores of the time, that part was a functional thing. These gates are not embellishments. They are part and parcel of fortress building at that time. And these are rather tame compared to a whole lot of others elsewhere.

Usually, they bore the name of the direction in which they were going. But not here. Why was it called the Maurepas Gate? And another, Frederic Gate—because they're the same man. He was Frédéric de Maurepas, the Pontchartrain Comte de Maurepas. He was the Minister of the Navy—oh, he had lots of functions. He was the Grand Master of the king's household. He controlled France. And he was the one that we are in constant correspondence with here. So that would be an interesting thing to speculate on: how come he got two gates named after him? Whereas there was none after the king; there was one after his son, the Dauphin Gate. We understand how that came. The king had had several daughters, and he was hankering for a son, and finally he got one. So there was a big celebration. And they were planning the gate in that year, so it became the Porte Dauphine in his honour. There's a little wee gate called the Queen's Gate, that was on the other side. Now, why did the queen get such a small gate to her name? Poor Queen Mary, she was a shy kind of girl; all she did was make kids for the king. She took a second seat; she wasn't very outgoing. She was the daughter of the king of Poland, who was exiled in eastern France because he had lost the throne of

Poland. And they needed a royal personnage to marry the king.

There are some ghost stories starting to come around here. People have been hearing things, have been seeing things, over the last several years. One day, somebody saw a person in a red costume coming, and they thought it was me. The people who saw him did not recognize his face, or see it very much. I'm not too sure. Because those stories, you know, they sort of grow. There's also somebody hearing things, steps in the house — in the Duhaget house. In the bakery, the baker one day swore he felt a presence behind him and saw something. It's all things that could be imagination, there's no doubt about that. But anyway, I hear that, and I say, Geez, wouldn't I like to see one, to talk to him, because I'd like to know this; it's either of two things. Either our work is so good that they feel at home. Or it's so bad that they're coming to haunt us. So I'd dearly like to know.

I'd like to come back in 50 or 100 years. To see how this thing has lived. Because right now, you see, the reality of Louisbourg is this one, not that one from the past. It's this one, because it's here and it's living. With all its problems, its present-day conditions. And this is the one which is interesting to me, to see what will have happened to it, how it will have lived over the time, how it will have adapted. One thing that I can see is that in time it will become interpreted completely in English, in its English reality, which is the "now" one. Which starts with the sieges. It's just a feeling I have. Because when you come to think of it, all this heritage business — nobody has any heritage from Louisbourg, nobody at all. It's meaningless. Except to, maybe, the descendants of the New Englanders. They are the ones who have ancestors buried here, who came and suffered here, and died here. Maybe the descendants of some of the French ones, too. We Acadians, we have no real heritage here. Canada doesn't, because this is a very short interlude of French history, and is only connected with Acadia in a by-the-way sort of thing, because the Acadians were up there in Nova Scotia, and traded with Louisbourg. And only a few came to settle in Cape Breton.

The ones who have really close feelings are those Americans. So, to me, that is the reality of Louisbourg. And I would be willing to bet that in 50 or 100 years, that will be the one which will have taken over. It has been rebuilt as much as possible as a French thing — that's fine. But with the other thing superimposing itself on it. (*In what way?*) That it becomes lived in by English-speaking people, who can handle it and tell the story. I illustrate it this way. When a study has been made of a certain subject, they're taken mostly from French text sources, and then digested, made into a report. And then when they need to be done in French, they are regurgitated in French from the English intermediate. And that shows. It shows in the form of the language that comes out, as well as into the thing itself. It cannot but be so.

You've heard him called Captain de Gannes here. That is a thing which is not French at all. You don't say "Captain de Gannes" in French. You say, "Monsieur de Gannes, Capitaine." So that when you hear it, it sounds English. A very subtle little thing which grates. A thing seen by English eyes being put into French by — unfortunately in Canada here, by the very nature of things — translation, reflects English. So, what comes back there, and comes out — an English-seen kind of thing, and an English-felt kind of thing. So it cannot but gradually go in time and become the richest part of the interest. It cannot be anything else.

HERE IS THE DUGAS HOUSE. He's the only Acadian, really, that settled here from Acadia. He was a carpenter. And his wife was a Richard girl. And after that she married a la Tour, Saint-Etienne de la Tour.

(*Did you have a great deal to go on when you did that house?*) To build the house, we found the foundation, which was fairly insubstantial. We were sure it was not a stone house. Now, as far as *charpente*, we deduced that from the fact that there was a foundation wall. But the rest is imagination. The *piquet* fill, for instance, that is our own thing. We didn't know. We put some *piquet* fill because the foundation was sort of light. And since there was the occupied upstairs, we presumed that there would have been a knee wall, therefore, the roof a bit higher. And since he was a carpenter, we thought we might try to give something special to his house. So we have put the *piquets* at an angle within the *charpente* framework, in the knee wall, just for a little change. Because having pieces like that in the framing members is quite common in many French frame houses. We thought, well, maybe Dugas re-

The Dugas house

membered that. But we don't know at all. This is purely our own thing. It's a pity, because everybody sort of likes it. We thought we could take this little liberty as a plausible thing that might have happened. And it might have been, but I wish I knew if it was really so.

(*You're aware of an inventive art, but at the same time, you're determined to get it as right as you can.*) Well, that's the challenge, you see, that I gave myself. Because, from an architecture point of view, it's not worth much, if you take architecture in its sort of superficial way—the design visual and all that sort of thing. But from a thing of reconnecting with the people of the past, with real people—the challenge I give myself is to reflect as close as possible what I can make of it, either by finding out or by re-inventing. That is why some imagination comes in. And creation, too. (*You read and then you try to apply that when you deal with these buildings.*) It's not so much that I try to it, but I figure that all that is there, and somehow I hope it will come through in the making of decisions and in the making of how I feel about the whole thing. I manage to get a little of that feeling through—very, very, very little, I'm afraid—but maybe more than I think.

While not being great architecture by any means, or exceptional or anything like that, it's extremely interesting. Because it's a good example of vernacular, quite functional. And it's amazing the number of French architects, especially the ones connected a little bit with historical architecture, are quite taken by the simple kind of functionalism and classical look about it.

Magnificent Obsessions

Because it was built-in at that time, a sense of architecture, in a sort of unconscious kind of way. Rhythm. See, they're not carefully, consciously designed. But they're made with a sense of the form, of the shape. A sense of form that was innate in people. Many, many people have a natural sense of the placing of things. That is the difference between our young civilization and a much older one. So, no, it's not great architecture by any means, but it is interesting.

Some of my architect friends in Moncton think I'm nuts, getting into this foolish thing. But I said, I've had the best of two worlds. I've had ten years private practice in Moncton and I've had this. But it was easier for me, going into this, because I already had some of the other one. I didn't have to worry about what I would do in ordinary architecture afterward. I wouldn't be good for it at all, now. I'm ruined!

Rue Toulouse looking toward the Frederic Gate

12

Mi'kmaq Godparents

Murdena Marshall

THE BOND BETWEEN *nkekunit* and *nklnikn* is limitless, it is one of the rarest and most beautiful gifts from the Creator. It is still very much respected today. So when Christianity came to our shores in the Sixteenth Century, Godparenting was not a new concept of the Mi'kmaw world. Beside all the responsibilities that *kkekunit* (*your* godparent) had, only one more was added, teaching Christian beliefs. The Mi'kmaw child did not lose anything but actually gained much more, including one more much loved *kkekunit*, from the opposite sex. Now

137

children have two or more persons to water their well-being in the tribal and Christian worlds.

The word *nkekunit* (my godparent) literally translates "s/he has me in his/her possession, I belong to him/her." *Nklnikn* (my godchild) translates into "my pillar of strength, my strength lies with her/him, my stronghold."

Prior to European contact, the Mi'kmaw family is generated by the extended family—the activities of the extended family. That your parents didn't have the sole responsibility of your upbringing. That other people within your family also had a role in educating you and in making you into a good productive individual. And those are your grandparents, on both sides, on your mother's side and your father's side—had a hand. They're the ones that really—from the formative years, which are four, five, six—had the most influence on you. Because you spent the greatest amount of time with them. Since your parents were always out gathering food and doing stuff to keep the elders and the children fed. So the adults spent most of their time hunting, getting food for their families.

So you spent your greatest amount of time with your grandparents when you were growing up. From them you learned about your whole history. You learn about how to run a household. Girls were taught how to run households, how to take care of siblings. Boys were taught little things—how to be a hunter—from their grandfathers. Through play, and through interaction.

But there was another individual in your life who had a lot of influence on you. And that was your other—well, your guardian. The "godparents" name just was Christianized. But prior to European contact, we had someone within the community who you could turn to if you were in trouble, if you were unhappy. You know, there was somebody for you that's yours. And that you're identified with that person. And that person's very important to you. Just as important as your parents. And just as important as your grandparents. It may be one of your aunts. Or it could be—someone from the community.

The language tells us that they were from the same gender. That a girl had a woman mentor, and the boy had a male mentor.

Mi'kmaq Godparents

But when a girl says "godparent" in her language, automatically it springs into the mind of the listener that (the godparent is a woman)—mental picture of a woman comes into view because the person who's uttered that word's a woman. And same with a boy.

Well, anyway, this mentor or this person is picked by your parents, way before you are born. They look at community members and look for qualities in community members. And who would make a good parent or good godparent if something should happen to us in early life. Or if something happens to our grandparents. Or if something happens that the whole family's wiped out and there's only the surviving kid.

So they look at the community as a whole and pick out an individual. They pick out two individuals. Because the baby's not born yet. And they're asked—both of these prospective godparents are asked if they would consider being a godparent.

Now, they're asked. And in some cases, even the godparent themselves come to the house and ask if they could possibly have the honour of being the godparents. In some cases. But in most cases it was the parents go and ask.

So when the baby's born—if it's a girl, the male mentor is out of the picture, temporarily. And concentration is held on the godmother, if it's a girl. And from your early age, from the time you can remember, you are always told that you have a godparent. And that this godparent is a good person. You always hear positive things about your godparent; there are never negative things. That this godparent is there for you if you ever need. And the bond is very, very, very, very, very evident in between godparent and godchild, even today. And as soon as the baby's born, this godparent comes often and there's a bonding between the baby and the godparent. And that bonding continues through life.

If you are a girl, the godparent is the one that tells you about your puberty age, you know, what happened to you when you become a woman. She'll be able to explain to you rationally, you know, she'll be able to do it without embarrassment because she is not your mother and she is not your grandmother, but someone who's neutral. So you're able to ask these questions that you won't be able to ask your parents, your mother or your grandmother. She prepares you for puberty. And she works with you at the celebrations and all that stuff. She even helps with the feast.

And as you grow up, if you are a rotten kid and you're unable to be disciplined by either grandparents or your parents, or they don't want to do it—the godparent is summoned. And the godparent takes you for a long walk. And she disciplines you or talks to you about your problem. She's able to look at you objectively when your parents can't or when your grandparents can't. Because she's not in the household herself and she doesn't know the circumstances. But she can talk to you as an individual, you know, why you shouldn't do these things.

So she straightens you out, gives you counselling.

And that goes on through life. It doesn't stop when you become puberty or when you're a teenager. It continues through life. Continues right to the end. And your godparent is just as important as your parent. And it generates from you the same sort of respect as you give to your parents. And that bonding is still evident today.

If you ever go to Eskasoni and look at Goli-Vision—we have our own cable TV. You will see, "To my godchild, happy birthday—love, godparent." You know. You'll see that all the time. Or something happens to the kid and they'll say, "Congratulations. Love, your godparent." You know? They don't put names, just say "godparent," because the child knows who the godparent is. It doesn't matter if the community doesn't know. It doesn't matter. The one that matters is between the kid and the godparent.

It was Christianized, of course, when baptism came about. But we received another godparent. Like—a girl received another godparent, which is a man. But that bonding isn't heavy. The bonding is between the same sex. (*At baptism they usually have a man and a woman stand for the child?*) Yeah. (*As the godparents.*) As the godparents. That's the Christian form. (*But the true bonding....*) Is with the same sex. Same sex.

The godparent does a lot of things for you. It's just not just earlier in life you're told if you need help, your godparent is there.... If something happens to me, your godparent is there. If you need

Mi'kmaq Godparents

anything, your godparent is there. And you utilize your godparent a lot, as you grow up. And the bond is just unbelievable.

(*Do you have a godparent?*) I have a godparent, yeah. She lives in Sydney River. Her name is Mary Kendall. And it's just unbelievable, the bonding that happens between....
(*She's been your godparent all your life.*) All my life.

(*Are you free to tell me how a godparent worked—something that happened that she played a role in?*)

Murdena's godparent, Mary Kendall

She was my mother's first cousin, first of all. And the way I used to hear about my godmother when I was small, that she was very gentle, and she was a good singer. So I always heard that when I was growing up, that my godmother was very very pretty, and she's a good singer. (*Oh, she wouldn't necessarily be around you all the time.*) Oh, yeah, oh, yeah. But I'm just telling you what I'd hear. I'd be hearing this as well. But my godmother moved away for a short period of time. She went to live in the United States for awhile. And when she came back it just—the bonding just—like it had never left off, it had never stopped.

It's a very, very beautiful—I don't how we'd call it, honest to God. It's just something that's unique. Although it has a Christian name to it, when you say it in English—godparent. But in Mi'kmaq, it's just said: my stronghold. (*What's the Mi'kmaw word?*) Nkekunit. You know, it's my stronghold. They have me, they're holding me up or whatever.

(*Can you remember your godmother taking you for a walk?*) Oh, yes. Even when she came back from the United States, she looked me up right away. To me, she's special. She is special to me because I know she must have been a good person before my mother could have possibly picked her. So I know she's a good person because of that. And I know there was something between her and my mother that made her my godparent, my godmother.

And through her I see my mother—my mother died when I was seven. But she always talks about my mother. When we talk, she'll always tell me stories about my mother. You know, she takes me back to my childhood and talks about my mother. Which I lack, because she died when I was very young. So she's able to fill that gap, the gap that my mother vacated in terms of activities. You know, what would she be like if we went to a ball game, what would she be like going to a card game.

So she is able to fill in all those little mazes, that were mazes to me at first, but now they're actual paths. It's a beautiful bonding. And that's not between just my godmother and I—that's with every godparent in the Mi'kmaq world. This is the bonding that's between godparent and the child.

(*Are you able to give me examples, how godparents have served for other people? Someone who may have gotten into serious trouble...?*) Well, when my kids were growing up, when I couldn't discipline them myself, or I was unable to discipline them, unruly teenagers as they were, in the '80s, '70s and '80s—I always contacted their godparents and just said, "Could you please talk to my son. He's getting unruly." And my son's godparent, who's also my first cousin—I'd see him drive down his driveway and go right into our house, and just point to him. You know, "Come." And my son would drop everything and go with him. And then he's getting counselling while they're out.

And sometimes, I guess, just having someone to talk to without being subjective. Like a godparent is able to listen to your side of the story for once, and doesn't make the judgment. When things happen in the household, of course, you're splitting—"No, that's his fault." "No, they started that." You know. But a godparent is not present and is unaware of what's happening in the household. But is able only to listen to what the kid has to say. And from there they work together.

(*Do we have stories tied to the godparent?*) I don't know, really. I don't imagine we do. But they're so evident. They're so real—godparents are so real that they haven't been able to be put in a legend. Because if you can put something in a legend, then you start off with the words *ke'skw a*, which means a long, long time ago. But godparent—the concept of godparenting is well and alive. So you couldn't put it in that context. Could never put it in that context. See? I have not heard any legends about godparents. Because they're here, they're here....

SEE, MOST GODPARENTS KNEW YOUR PARENTS in a positive way. I mean, a parent wouldn't pick a person who they're in conflict with in any way, shape, or form. So first of all, the relationship between a parent and a godparent has to be very smooth and good. So that smoothness and goodness just continues with the relationship with the child. There's no conflict—there's no room for conflict of any sort. No different beliefs—knowing that you're on the same track all the time as your parents are. Godparent is always on the same medium as your parents are.

(It's the fundamental idea that seems so important. Just in that you could have someone else that's not the police. Someone else that's not a psychiatrist. At the moment when things are difficult.) Momentary. They're able to be fixed up.

Even when you're an adult. When you have problems in your marriage. And you can't go to your parents, because sometimes your parents will tell you, "Well, you made your bed, now lie in it." But a godparent can look at both sides—can look at you, and look at your husband, and look at your children. And able to put them all in the same bowl and stir them up. When your parents sometimes will take your side. In most cases parents will take the husband's side, because that's what Mi'kmaw life is. If I go to my father and complain about my husband. "Well," he'd tell me, "I think Albert is right." They don't comfort you in the fact that you're going to leave him. Unless it's very evident that he's abusing you and that he's running around with 20 other women and all that stuff. In most cases, if there's an argument within the family and you run home to your parents, they'll tell you he's probably right. So you don't want to talk to your parent, because—you know what's coming, anyway!

So what the godparent does is look at it—the godparent can look at both sides of the coin and able to spin it and hope it falls on the right side. And that's the beauty of a godparent. That's

Magnificent Obsessions

the beautiful duty of a godparent. (*And a beautiful element of Mi'kmaw culture.*) It is. (*And still alive.*) And very much alive. Very much alive. Very much alive.

So alive that even some parents won't allow you to marry their godchild. Because of that closeness between perhaps your father and his godson, and that he sees his godson as a son. And deep down in the back of his mind there is the word incest floating about. In some cases even they'll want to discourage you. And they'll tell you from the time that you bring this young fellow home, "Listen, that's my godson." And that's how strong that is. It's so evident. And you know, in reality, you can marry this guy if you want to, that there's no reason why you can't. But morally, your parents feel that that's your dad's godson. That's important. And in that way, the father is worried. If an argument should ever happen between this couple, and the godson comes to him, "How could I be possibly objective when he's married to my daughter?"

Murdena Marshall is an Elder from Eskasoni Mi'kmaq First Nation, and a retired professor of Mi'kmaq Studies at Cape Breton University. The opening paragraph is taken from Murdena Marshall's explanation in the *Micmac News*, October 1991.

13

A Cape Breton Tea Ceremony

Lori Cox

EXCHANGE RELATIONS in mainstream society are almost entirely governed by written contracts and monetary considerations. We even set up relationships within our family on a contract basis. We pay our children to wash the windows or mow the lawn. We give them an allowance that depends on certain chores getting done. Many people believe that this teaches children responsibility and how to live in the world. But this is a different world from the one that existed in Cape Breton in 1971, the year that the Black Point community in northern Cape Breton was closed.

In 1971, the frolics were a thing of the past but people still helped each other plant

potatoes and make hay and launch their boats. Afterwards they sat in the kitchen, drank tea, shared something to eat, and exchanged stories, jokes and songs. The old forms had been adapted. The following accounts are taken from observations in a journal I've kept.

Where Everyone Knows That "No" Means "Yes

IN THE BAY DISTRICT–the Bay St. Lawrence region of Cape Breton–it is customary to offer guests tea when they come to visit. This seemingly spontaneous behaviour is actually quite prescribed and formal. The social obligations that are very much a part of the tea ritual and the set of rules that guide the whole transaction became apparent to me when someone in the community didn't follow them. The rules governing the behaviour towards people in the immediate family and kinship group are different. The tea ritual that I am describing is the one that I observed most often. So it must be understood that these are the "rules" and the forms defined when a person is not located within the kinship group.

R.C., a young man of 25, told me that a woman, J., in a neighbouring community was "mean," the local term for stingy, because she didn't serve him tea. He was visiting the family because his father had picked up something for them in Sydney, a small city about 120 miles from the Bay. Northern Cape Breton continues to be quite isolated. There are few services available in the area and often people have to drive to Sydney to buy a pair of shoes or to go to the dentist. For many years there was a small bus service that operated a few days a week but the government cut the small subsidy that enabled the bus to operate.

R.C. was delivering something. The woman invited him in; they chatted for a while and then she offered him tea. But, he complained to me that she never made him tea.

This seemed very unusual and I asked him to explain. He told me that when she had offered him tea he had refused. He believed she should have brought him the tea anyway, and that she had treated him rudely. I remember laughing at him. It seemed perfectly reasonable to me that, if he told her that he didn't want tea, then she wouldn't think that she should give him tea. My perspective,

146

however, was not the perspective of the community at that time.

R. C. knew that for some reason the woman wasn't following the rules. She may have considered him a child and not an adult because children usually are more direct. If they say they want a cookie when they are asked no one thinks it rude, nor do they think it rude if they refuse to accept. The answer to her question "Would you like a little tea?" was supposed to be "No." Usually, "No, thank you. I've just eaten"—because it is also understood that tea meant a "little lunch." In Northern Cape Breton "tea" was never just tea. It was understood as tea and something to eat, a "little lunch." I overheard a conversation between three older men who had worked in various places. One said that people up in Sydney were "mean" because when they offered a person tea they just brought out tea and nothing but tea. They all agreed. One of the other men remarked that people in P.E.I. were the meanest he'd ever met because he'd been working there and the people he met didn't even invite a person in for tea. In Northern Cape Breton, however, [saying "No" to tea] is pure social deception.

The host is supposed to ignore that guest's "No, thank you" and to begin the preparations for tea. The table might be set, the food prepared, and the boiling water poured into the teapot. The water on the stove would usually be boiling at this point because at the first sight of a visitor the kettle is filled with water and moved over to boil on the stove.

When tea is served it is proper not to refuse it. There is, however, no real pressure put on the guests to eat—as there might be in a Jewish or Italian household. The tea cup is kept filled and guests are encouraged to eat as much as they want. "Have some more tea. Have some more bread. Have some more scones." The visitor refuses but the hostess keeps the plate and the cup filled.

There seems to be a whole mode of behaviour that defines visiting. Guests always enter through the kitchen even if there is a front door to the house, Guests remove their shoes in the porch if there is one and enter without knocking. If there is no porch they simply walk in and remove their shoes by the door. The kitchen is the place where people gather.

Usually, the host will remark that there is no need to take off the boots or shoes; but the visitor will take them off anyway. The guests walk directly into the doorway but not into the house. They stand by the door until they are invited in and asked to sit down. Guests rarely take their coats off and will often sit for hours with them on no matter how warm the kitchen is. Visitors are encouraged, however, to take their coats off through the entire visit. The proper response is to say that it is time to go.

"There's plenty of time," the host will say throughout the visit, no matter how late or how long a guest has stayed. When the hostess asks about tea, visitors usually will make a motion that they are just getting ready to leave. But at this point the hostess usually has the tea just about made. Visitors also might make a motion to leave before they have been asked but this is a signal for the hostess to inquire if the guest would like something. If she doesn't, then her husband might say "A cup of tea would be nice." If there are older girls in the household, they might be asked to fix tea. But it is usually more of a command. "Give the woman a cup of tea," as if to remind them of their duty. The food accompanying tea can be anything from a light meal to a plate full of cookies and cakes to bread or bannock and molasses or jam.

There was a sense of plenty and abundance that accompanied tea. There was plenty of tea, plenty of time, and certainly plenty of scones. The whole encounter seemed to be completely spontaneous and there was never a sense of any kind of obligation to the patterns that everyone expected.

These patterns really defined people's behaviour and also their expectations of the behaviour of other people in the community. But they allowed enough variation so people could use them to express their thoughts and feelings about the other person. The variations were all meaningful. How a person offered tea or when they offered it. How many times the tea cup was filled and what kind of food was provided—all of these were signs that could communicate exactly what people thought and felt about each other.

PEOPLE COULD CHOOSE TO DISREGARD these rules entirely but their reputations were at stake. They were considered "mean" if they chose not to give and rude if they chose not to receive. Visitors were never in so much of a rush when they came on business that they didn't stay at least for a little while and visit.

In these exchanges the social relations seemed to take precedence over any economic or material necessity. This may have been an illusion, but it worked. In visiting and taking tea, people were able to take care of business but at the same time they communicated quite subtly and gracefully the nature of their relationships. They also had the freedom to decide whether or not they wanted to strengthen or weaken the bonds of their relationship.

Purpose and Pretence: Borrowing and Lending

THE PURPOSE SERVED by the social deception involved in these encounters might not be immediately apparent to an outsider who would think it strange that people said "no" when really they meant "yes."

The guests' refusal may have been an illusion, but it was a graceful way of giving the hosts the freedom to offer whatever it was they had or chose to give. As Marcel Mauss found in the communities that he studied, whatever gift was being given must always seem to be "freely given." There were also three obligations: to give, to receive and to reciprocate.

Most exchanges in Northern Cape Breton took this form and many still do. For instance, often when someone comes to visit, there is a reason; but often that reason is not immediately or directly stated. This is true even if they came for something quite specific, to borrow a ladder, to get some information, or to ask for help. The request that is made is translated into the form of the exchange pattern.

When L., my neighbour, came to visit, I knew, because it was the middle of the day, that he probably came for a particular reason. I was busy working in the garden. Dennis, my mate, wasn't home. I took the vegetables that I had picked and we both went to the house. As we were talking I was trying to figure out from the conversation what he had come for. I made tea and tried to ask the questions that would reveal the reason for his visit.

He seemed totally relaxed as if he had all the time in the world.

His only concern seemed to be that he was taking me away from my work. The conversation continued spiraling in smaller and smaller circles until after awhile we reached the necessity that had carried him to my kitchen. He told me that he and his son had been putting new shingles on their roof. We talked about wood shingles and asphalt shingles and the merits and cost of both. We talked about Oddie [Audie] Morrison in Cape North who used to have a shingle mill and also about the mill still operating in Scotsville.

I wondered if he had run out of shingles or tar and mentioned that it was hard to know exactly how much material to order. I wondered if he was inquiring if we were going into Sydney soon, so we could pick him up more supplies, or whether he thought we might have some extra shingles, because we had just finished building. I mentioned that we were going into Sydney that weekend. We talked briefly about the bus to Sydney not operating. But that conversation didn't go anywhere.

Then he started talking about the weather being great for shingling. He hoped that he would be able to finish the job while they had such a good spell of weather. The weather had to be dry and cool enough to make it possible to work on the roof but warm enough so that the tabs of tar on the shingles stuck. We discussed how important it was to put extra tar under the shingles because in our area there are extremely high winds. I asked how long he thought the job might take. He said that he really didn't know at this point. They couldn't reach the peak of the roof with their ladder, so they might have to build some staging.

He needed our long aluminum extension ladder. He still didn't ask, though. He started to tell a funny story about a local woman known as "Big Theresa" whose roof was leaking and needed to be fixed; she ended up fixing it herself without her husband's assistance. When he was finished, I told him that we had a long extension ladder that might reach where he needed to go. At first he refused. He wouldn't want to take it, he said, if we needed it. I assured him that we weren't working at anything vaguely connected with a ladder. He was also close by if we did need it. What was unspoken was all of the help that he had given us in the past. All of the tools we'd borrowed and all of the times he'd taught us how to do something. He said that if it was no trouble "that would be great" and then after a quick "tea" and a few more funny stories we went out to the barn to get the ladder.

This kind of encounter, filled as it was with gift exchanges, was extremely enlightening for me. He came to ask me about the ladder, but we exchanged tea, stories, lunch, and gifts. Actually, there was a kind of continuous exchange going on with our neighbour, so the reciprocality between us had little to do with a feeling of owing something specific or measurable. I didn't feel obligated to lend him the ladder simply as a payback because he had loaned us his bob sled last winter. The obligations that I felt were real but they were more like the ties of family than those of business.

I had been taught to be much more direct in my exchanges with people. I had been taught that people shouldn't waste other people's time. Time was like money and there was never enough of it. In this community, however, there was no sense of "wasting" or "spending" time. Instead people "passed the time."

My response and manner may not be typical of the community pattern, but in some sense it was shaped by my neighbour's way of relating. I couldn't be direct because this would simply reduce his visit to business. This certainly wasn't the nature of our relationship. To some people it might seem that the ladder was the real purpose of the exchange. But the ladder was merely another token of the currency of mutual affection that flowed more or less continuously between our households. This is not to say that it wasn't important, but we both knew that it wasn't the most important thing between us.

So, in some way, the seeming lack of purpose is important. The exchange between us was able to unfold gracefully and the threads connecting us strengthened. In some sense we both let business take care of itself while we used the occasion to enjoy each other's company.

The Obligations of the Gift

BECAUSE THESE RULES ARE UNWRITTEN, though, it was difficult to understand them until, out of ignorance, we broke one of them. One winter afternoon our horses broke out of the fence and ran off down the road. We couldn't locate them, but that evening they made their way to a neighbour's, J. He lived in the village itself, which was about five miles away from us. It was a cold evening and one of the horses, a young mare, leaned up against his warm kitchen window and cracked one of the panes of glass. J. called us up and told us that our horses were at his place. He never mentioned the broken glass. We came and got the animals and it was then that we found out about the damage. We offered to pay him but he refused. We offered again but he still refused. What we didn't realize, though, was that this refusal was something of an illusion. It wasn't that he wanted the money. As Mauss pointed out, in these exchanges the payment of the return "gift" is not immediate because there is a certain lack of respect in just paying people for a favour or a gift they have given you. The immediacy of the act belittles the expression of friendship that is implied in the original gift. So the return gift is deferred and this is a sign of a certain deference or respect.

But we didn't understand any of this. We just thought that he was being really nice. We also believed that he didn't want the money and we thought that he would be insulted if we pushed it on him. We were probably right, but he probably would have made allowances because we were from "away." It would have been better than what we did which was simply to thank him without bringing him a return gift. What we should have done was to bring him a roast of pork when we slaughtered our pig or to pick up a bottle of rum for him at Christmas. We thought that when he said "No," he didn't want anything for the window, that he really meant what he said.

So we never really thought too much about it until about a year later. We were at a little get together at our neighbour's and J. was drinking. Out of the blue he challenged Dennis, my mate, to a fight. I finally realized that it was over the window. J. felt extremely insulted at our behaviour. We learned that it wasn't really the cost of the window. He didn't want payment as such. But he thought that if we cared for him we would have brought him some "gift" as a token of appreciation of his generosity and friendship. By not taking our money for the window he had in some sense given it as a gift to us. We should have honoured this generosity and the connection he had initiated in some more formal and material way than simply by saying thank you. We ended up insulting J. without meaning to because we didn't really understand the pretense that is often involved in these social exchanges.

This is not to say that people "lie" to each other because sometimes they say "no" when they mean "yes." Everyone knows what is happening. It is like being thirsty and wanting a drink, but learning to go to the end of the line and take your turn. It is simply part of a larger form that allows a certain spaciousness to be part of the exchanges between people. People who feel as if they have room don't mind sharing some of it with the people around them. It allows people a freedom, because exchanges almost always take the form of "giving and receiving" rather than "owing and taking."

The form does entail a certain kind of illusion and deception because people do have economic and social obligations that are tacitly understood, that is, there is a principle of reciprical-ity at work. But people choose whether or not they are going to fulfill what they or others might perceive as their obligations. For instance, a direct question, "Will you lend me your ladder?" demands an immediate reply and there is compulsion in this. When questions are posed indirectly, it allows for the form of I give this to you as a gift. I give not because you demand it of me or because I owe it to you but because I offer it to you freely, because I honour you, because I respect you, because I am your friend and your neighbour. This freedom is not decep-tion because I can still choose not to "give." This refusal may be read as an insult but there is actually room within the form to refuse in a manner that is graceful. What is at stake is really the honour and reputation of the people giving and the people receiving. So there is much room allowed in every exchange for expressing respect and regard. What impresses me always is the gracefulness of exchanges that follow this form and a certain sense of freedom and lack of compulsion or push.

The whole system of relations revolves around generosity. This is not to say that exchanges are entirely devoid of self-interest. It's just that they have little to do with simple economic self-interest or utility. What is always at stake is a person's honour and worth, not only on a public but also on a private level. Marcel Mauss mentioned the importance of the public display of generosity in the groups that he studied. In many of these everyday exchanges in the Bay district, there is not always a big public display involved. But the community is small enough that people do tend to know almost everything about each other's activities. There is also a kind of personal honour at stake, that seems just as important as what other people think — that is what you think of yourself and what you do.

In the traditional Black Point family generosity is valued more highly than anything else. As A. MacKinnon said, "If I have it and you need it, if I don't give it then something is wrong with me." This leads sometimes to a kind of extravagance in giving, which Mauss also reported.

Extravagant Exchange

WHEN THE TRANSMISSION WENT in our old truck one winter, A. MacKinnon said that he had one that we could borrow. He told us that he would need it back in the spring, though, because it was the transmission from his lobster fishing boat. But, he said, we were welcome to use it all winter.

He never considered the wear and tear on the transmission nor the fact that it might even break while we were using it. He never considered that, if it did break, we might not be able to replace it and then he would be unable to fish. Or, if he did consider it, he never told us about it.

Implicit in his offering us the gift of his transmission was the trust and faith in our friendship but also his faith in the whole system itself. His act had social meaning. He was communicating to us and to the community that we were more important than the transmission. And that he honoured us as friends.

But he also had a certain faith that he wouldn't lose. He had no assurances, though, just faith in his friends and neighbours. Mauss found that in this system people rarely are impoverished by the gifts they give, even when they give away everything that they own. Because they also receive extravagantly. Mauss reported an extravagant feast that was part of the birth ceremonies that were performed by the new parents in Samoa. They received numerous birth presents from the guests and they were actually left no richer or poorer than they were before the feast. But, he said, "They had the satisfaction of seeing what they considered to be a great honour, namely the heaps of property collected in the occasion of the birth of their child" [from Marcel Mauss, *The Gift*, 1967, pages 6-7].

Although A. MacKinnon's offer of a transmission might seem foolish from a mainstream perspective it makes perfect sense in this light. Traditionally, there is no value placed on the individual accumulation and ownership of material goods or on people's ability to display their wealth. Success has to do more with people's willingness to dispose of their wealth, to give it away to their friends, to spend it as a mark of honour and respect.

Things are changing in the Bay district, but only a few years ago, when the engine did go in A. MacKinnon's boat, a mechanic who had experienced his incredible generosity, took a leave from his job, traveled more than a hundred miles, and stayed with A.'s family for a week, to help rebuild the engine, free of charge, so that A. could go fishing.

The Circle Of Giving

IF A PERSON RECEIVED A GIFT, there was a responsibility to give in turn. But, again, this was not necessarily in the form of direct reciprocality between two individuals. You give this to me and this means that I have to give something of equal value to you.

When we were building our first house, we brought our logs to a man who owned a small saw mill. His father had been a sawyer before him. Neither of them did this as a business. They simply milled up logs when they needed them or when their

Magnificent Obsessions

neighbours did. Because two people were needed in the operation usually the person who brought the logs would help him do the milling. The person was charged a small amount of money for each board foot of lumber that was milled. This covered the cost of operating the mill and perhaps a little extra.

After our logs were sawed we went to pay the man but he refused the money. Because this was a recognized transaction we knew that there was no insult involved in giving him money. We insisted but he refused. We tried to leave it on the kitchen table when we left but he came out to our truck and gave us back the money. Then he told us this story.

When he was young, he said, and was building his first house, he brought his logs to a man to saw them because his mill wasn't set up at the time. When he went to pay, though, the sawyer wouldn't take any money. The sawyer told him that when he, in his time, had been building his first house the man who milled up his logs had also refused to take payment. He told him that he couldn't repay the man the favour because he was dead, but that he was passing it along to him.

Our neighbour told us that he, in turn, was passing it along to us. We were honoured and we felt as if we were filled with an energy that we also wanted to keep alive. When we killed our chickens that fall we made sure to bring him enough for the winter. But this had little to do with material reciprocity or obligation. We didn't feel that we were repaying a debt, that is, giving him the chickens to pay back for the milling of the logs. Instead we were honouring the relationship and his friendship and, in our turn, bestowing a gift. His gift to us and his story explaining it also nurtured a certain kind of awareness in us that helped to shape our relationship to everyone in the community.

This chapter is edited from Lorraine Vitale Cox's doctoral thesis, *Engineered Consent: The Relocation of Black Point, A Small Gaelic Fishing Community in Northern Cape Breton Island.* 1997. Lori presently works in Elsipogotg First Nation and is devoted to the Nogemag Initiative that explores approaches to wellness and education that are grounded in the M'igmag community culture but replicable in diverse populations. She still spends one-sixth of her life in Cape Breton, the home of her heart.

14

"So How Do You Get the Rope Up?"

Clarence Barrett

W E HAD PULLED IN SOMEWHERE to a roadside picnic table for lunch and struck up a conversation with a traveler from Quebec named Marcel. He asked about places to hike on the Island and the conversation turned to hiking and climbing in Quebec. I had made a couple of climbing trips there and was impressed by the quality and extent of the granite walls and slabs. Marcel was eager to do some climbing on his visit to Nova Scotia so we arranged to meet next day at the Grande Falaise, a cliff located near the highway a few kilometres north of the Petit Etang entrance to the

Magnificent Obsessions

Cape Breton Highlands National Park. It was one of my favourite climbing areas and I had often spent days exploring its gullies and buttresses, sometimes lingering just below the summit on summer evenings to watch the sun set over the Gulf of St. Lawrence.

According to geologists this rock formation was once on the other side of the highlands but has been thrust across the plateau by tectonic events on a lubricating base of gypsum, veins of which are visible on the cliff. Continual weathering has loosened tonnes of material from the cliff face which, under the influence of gravity, has formed an extensive scree slope leading up to the base of the cliff. The rocky slopes are home to a little creature known as the Gaspé shrew. It's been found in a few similar habitats in Cape Breton but the only other places in the world where it is known to exist are in the Gaspé and at a locality in northern New Brunswick.

I wonder how much of the cliff is buried in scree and if removing the rock would expose hidden routes and add another couple of hundred feet of good climbing. Until the next glacier scours the valley we would have to be content with what was there, which meant going through the take-two-steps-up-and-slide-one-step-back routine up the loose slope to get to the bottom of the climbs. After humping a load of rope, hardware, food and water up to the base of the cliff you usually felt you could levitate up the first pitch.

I should explain at this point the basic climbing procedure and try to answer a frequently asked question: "How do you get the rope up?" One way, of course, is to walk up the back side of the hill to the top of the cliff and lower one end of the rope to a climber on the ground. But apart from the ethical problem that this creates for some purists, not all peaks are accessible in this way or, like the Falaise, are too high for the rope to reach the ground. So other means have been developed.

Let's say Marcel decides to climb first. He ties one end of the rope to his harness and gets ready to climb. I tie the other end of the rope to a solid anchor (a big boulder or tree) near the start of the climb. After looping the rope around the boulder and tying it, I take something called a *carabiner* and fasten it to the end of the rope that's anchored to the boulder. A carabiner is an oval metal device that looks like a very big chain link except that it has a spring-loaded hinged gate along one side that can be opened and closed.

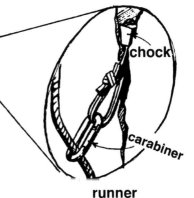

The rest of the rope between the
anchor and Marcel is laid in a
loose pile on the ground, free of
knots or tangles.
Marcel is ready to go but before
he starts, a por- tion of the rope that
he will be drag- ging off the top of
the pile is clipped into the carabiner
that's been se- cured to the anchor. The rope is
wrapped around the carabiner (by me) in such a
way that the cara- biner can function as a braking
device. By hold- ing the rope in a certain way
I can allow the rope to run through the braking
carabiner freely or I can easily stop it.
Marcel be- gins to climb. Standing beside
the anchored carabiner, through which the
rope is running, I control the rope, feeding
it through the carabiner as Marcel climbs.
Of course, if he were to fall now he would land
on the ground; there is nothing I can do to stop
him. If he was
up high enough
when he fell he
would get hurt,
so there must
be some way to
limit the dis-
tance he falls.
So shortly af-

chock

carabiner

braking device

runner

ter he starts climbing, when he gets about two or three metres off the ground, Marcel places a metal wedge called a chock into a crack in the cliff face just above him, in such a way that it cannot become dislodged. (For various reasons chocks have replaced the more traditional pitons that were hammered into cracks in the rock.) A short loop of rope (30 centimetres or so) extends from the chock, to which Marcel clips a carabiner. This set-up is called a runner.

While using his legs and one hand for balance and support he reaches down and grabs the rope that's trailing from his harness, lifts up some slack, and clips it into the runner carabiner. (Remember that the carabiner has a spring-loaded gate that can be opened to accept the rope.) Now the rope is coming off the top of the pile beside me, through my hands and the braking carabiner, up the cliff, through the runner carabiner and to Marcel's harness. Should he fall at this point I would apply the brake mode to the rope and he would be suspended by the rope which will be supported by the runner carabiner.

Marcel keeps climbing. You can see from the diagram that the farther he ascends above the runner the farther he will fall if he slips. So after climbing some distance beyond the first runner he places another runner. How high he climbs before placing the second runner depends on the difficulty of the route, his climbing ability and the availability of suitable places to anchor the runner. It's entirely up to his judgment. He keeps climbing and putting in runners for as long as he wants, as long as there is enough rope to continue. The rope is 45 meters (150 feet) long.

When he stops, probably at a ledge where he can rest, he sets up an anchor system similar to the one that was set up on the ground, including a braking carabiner, while I disassemble the one on the ground and tie into that end of the rope.

Now it's my turn to climb. As I ascend, Marcel takes the slack, pulling the rope through the braking carabiner at the new anchor site. If I slip at any point, Marcel puts on the brake and my fall is immediately arrested. As the second person up, I have a much easier go of it and can climb under a lot less physical and mental stress because I don't have to place secure runners with one hand while maintaining balance with the other, at some distance above the last runner. The only thing I have to worry about is how to retrieve the chocks that sometimes manage to get jammed or lodged deep in a crack. At each chock I come to I unclip the rope from it and collect it. If I need both hands to retrieve stubborn ones, I can actually hang suspended by the rope while Marcel applies the brake.

When I reach Marcel the normal procedure will be for me to continue climbing past him, taking over the lead and using the runners that I collected on the way up to protect my ascent. Thus we would alternate the lead, leapfrogging past one another until we reached the summit. Each segment of a climb is referred to as a *pitch*.

That, then, briefly describes the basic process. For the sake of simplicity I have omitted a lot of details. The act of safeguarding a climber as he or she climbs is called *belaying* them. You will notice that throughout this sequence the rope is *not* used to climb on, it merely acts as a safety line to hold a climber if he falls (which makes you wonder what the guy in the Marlboro ad is doing half way up a cliff with the coil of rope over his shoulder).

Over the years climbing gear has improved, resulting in routes of greater and greater difficulty being mastered. Modern ropes, for example, have a certain amount of built-in elasticity in order to absorb the impact that a falling climber places on the anchors and on his body. Chocks made of lightweight alloys are available in a multitude of shapes and sizes. Specialized footwear is available to match the nature of different kinds of rock.

But on that day, years ago, I was at the bottom of the second pitch of the Slab route, shod in secondhand army boots with nailed-on Vibram soles, carrying homemade pitons fashioned from scrap angle iron, a chock collection that included an assortment of ordinary machine nuts with the threads filed out of them, and 45 metres of marine hawser purchased at Sydney Ship Supply, the upper end of which had disappeared over a bulge in the rock above me and hadn't moved much in half an hour. After the first pitch Marcel had decided to continue leading but seemed to be having trouble finding places to put runners.

The rope had moved upward a couple of times and then lowered back down. An occasional shower of pebbles told me that he was clawing away at something but he didn't seem to be making much progress. Every once in a while a fist-sized piece of rock went sailing by and I watched till it hit the rocks below and took off on a new trajectory. A split-second later I would hear the crack and the smell of broken stone wafted up on the breeze.

"This stuff is awfully loose," he shouted as another piece plummeted by.

"You'll cover up the lower part of the face if you keep piling rocks down there. I think there's some kind of regulation about altering the landscape in a national park." I knew there were sections of loose rock but I didn't remember it being that bad.

I waited for a while longer. I was getting impatient because it was getting late in the day. But it wasn't boring, there was lots to see from up there: the coastal plain and the western edge of the highlands stretching away to the south, beyond the spire of the church in Chéticamp; the estuary and tidal channels of the river at Petit Etang; a goshawk circling over the Rigwash Valley; a raven's nest below me on the cliff.

Little cars kept driving into the parking lot and tiny people would get out, go over to the little square boxes in the trees, return to the cars and drive away. Some of them would stop long enough for the obligatory snapshot of the cliff. Occasionally someone would sit to admire the expanse of naked rock for a while and then you would see arms pointing up, binoculars would be brought out and a little crowd would gather. But most were unaware of our little adventure on the crags.

Harebells growing out of cracks in the rock nodded in the breeze. Rare arctic-alpine plants had been reported on some parts of the cliff. Whether there were any on the ledge or not I don't remember, but in taking stock of the different plants that were trying to make a living up there, I noticed that I was sitting beside a small patch of poison ivy.

I began to wonder if Marcel was off the route. Tying off the rope I backed up for a look. He was indeed lost and we hadn't even started up the most difficult centre wall. It was getting late in the day, big black clouds were starting to roll in and I wasn't keen on having to spend the night on the cliff. He suggested that

La Grande Falaise

I take over the lead since I was familiar with the route.

The wall is a wonderfully exposed piece of rock that starts about 30 metres up the cliff and rises vertically for another 30 metres, terminating in a broad ledge about two thirds of the way to the summit. By today's standards it would not be considered particularly difficult, but the exposure was great and it provided some exhilarating climbing.

From the top of the wall the route went over some easy rock until it came to a steep inside corner or gully formed where two faces came together like the pages of an open book. With the sound of thunder reverberating off the surrounding hills we quickly set up a belay anchor at the top of the wall and I headed off for the gully. As I started up the gully, bridging the sides with my legs and balancing with my hands, violent gusts of wind started coming up from below, lifting my nylon jacket up over my face. I began to feel like a kite.

Halfway up the gully—the heavens opened up. Great big spatter drops of rain pelted my hard-hat and in less than a minute I was soaked to the skin. The only thing to do was to keep going There was nothing to tie off to, the last runner was three metres below me and climbing down was out of the question. Just beyond the top of the gully I knew there was a spruce tree that would serve

163

as an anchor. If I could make it to that we would be home free. I placed two chocks in a rather dubious crack and kept going.

Three metres from the top of the gully I felt the rope draw taut.

Whenever we were out of earshot, we communicated with tugs on the rope. I gave two tugs to indicate that I wanted slack but there was no response. I waited a few seconds and gave another couple of tugs. Still no slack. I could hear Marcel shouting several times but couldn't make him out until, during a temporary lull in the wind, I heard the words "no more rope!"

What a revolting development. I had always made it to the top of this gully before without running out of rope but then it occurred to me that the year before I had cut five metres off the rope in order to get rid of a section that had started to fray. That five metres was all I needed to reach the top of the gully.

I couldn't stay there indefinitely. My legs were giving out. I gave three tugs on the rope, the pre-arranged signal that meant I had set up an anchor and was ready for Marcel to dismantle the anchor and braking system down below. Once he undid the rope from his anchor I would no longer be protected by the safety system, but I would have enough rope to get to the top of the gully. As soon as I felt the slack in the rope I started up.

Under the best conditions this particular pitch was dicey because of the lack of places to put chocks. Now everything was wet, the rain was coming down in sheets, the wind was buffeting from every direction and I thought that any minute I would either be blown off the rock or fried by lightning. It seemed that there were very few seconds between the flashes and the ear-splitting thunder. The only part of me that was dry was my mouth. I was flying on my own.

I reached the top of the gully but the only way to get out of it to the spruce tree was over a steep, slippery section of creeping shrubbery that didn't offer much to hang on to. But I could just reach some of the roots of the tree where it came close to the gully and was able to throw a piece of nylon sling around them and clip my harness to it. It wasn't very comfortable, since I was more or less suspended from the sling, dangling just below the top of the gully, but it was secure. With the braking carabiner clipped to my harness I could belay Marcel as he climbed up the gully and out to the summit.

The rain, of course, stopped shortly after we finished, as quickly as it had started. After catching our breath at the top we made our way through the woods at the edge of the cliff and scrambled down a shallow gully to the top of a long scree slope off to one side of the cliffs. With great leaps and bounds and wild whoops of celebration we "screed" almost all the way down to the highway.

Under the National Parks Act climbing is now prohibited on the Grande Falaise in order to preserve the rare plants that grow on the cliff face, but sometimes I pull in to the parking lot to look at the rock and to retrace the different routes in my mind. As someone once said, "Who has known heights shall not again know peace...."

Author of *Cape Breton Highlands National Park: A Park Lover's Companion*, Clarence Barrett loves undiscovered Cape Breton, and is generous with his enthusiasm for this island. He is a warden in the Cape Breton Highlands National Park.

Magnificent Obsessions

NOTES to
Irish Convicts Abandoned in Cape Breton, 1788

1 Letter from a British Regular Soldier, 5 August 1789 in *Report of the Department of Public Archives for the Year 1944*, p. xxxvii. National Archives of Canada (NAC) 1945, Dominion of Canada, Ottawa.

2 Shaw, A. G. L. *Convicts and the Colonies: A Study of Penal Transportation from Great Britain and Ireland to Australia and Other Parts of the British Empire*. Faber and Faber. London 1966 p. 25.

3 Ekirch, A. Roger. *Bound for America: The Transportation of British Convicts to the Colonies 1718-1775*. Clarendon Press. Oxford 1987 p. 27

4 *Ibid* p. 2.   5 *Ibid* p. 28.   6 *Ibid* p. 31.   7 *Ibid* p. 227.

8 *Ibid* p. 68.   9 *Ibid* p. 230.

10 Martin, Jed. Convict Transportation to Newfoundland in 1789. *Acadiensis* (Autumn) 1985 p. 65.   11 *Ibid* p. 85.

12 Frost, Alan. *Convicts and Empire: A Naval Question, 1776-1811*. Oxford University Press. Melbourne 1980 p. xv   13 *Freeman's Journal* 13-16 September 1788

14 *Ibid* 1-9 October 1788   15 *Ibid* 21-23 October 1788

16 Ekirch *Bound for America* p. 100

17 *Freeman's Journal* 13-16 September 1788   18 *Ibid* 16-18 October 1788

19 *Report of the Board of Trustees for the Year 1950*, Public Archives of Nova Scotia (PANS) King's Printer, Halifax. 1951 p. 18   20 *Ibid* p. 19

21 *Freeman's Journal* 3 January, 15-18 March, 6-9 September, 14-16 October, 9-12 August 1788   22 PANS p. 17   23 *Ibid* p. 20   24 *Ibid* p.22

25 Macarmick to Secretary of State Sydney, May 20 1788, in *Report of the Canadian Archives*, Public Archives of Canada (PAC) 1895 p. 23

26 PANS p. 25   27 *Ibid*   28 Taitt to Grenville, 9 March 1790, in Colonial Correspondence, originally C.O. 217, in a transcription at the Beaton Institute, UCCB as Cape Breton A, Vol 73, p. 1

29 Mathews to Macarmick, 30 March 1789, Cape Breton A, Vol. 73 p. 41

30 PANS p. 28   31 Grenville to Macarmick, 20 October 1789, Cape Breton A. PAC p. 24,33   32 PANS p. 37   33 PANS p. 38

34 *Freeman's Journal* 2-4 July 1789

35 Murdock, Beamish. *History of Nova Scotia or Acadie*. James Barnes. Halifax 1866 p. 74; PANS p. 19   36 Grenville to Macarmick, 20 October 1789, Cape Breton A

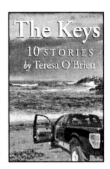

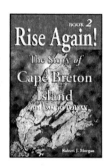
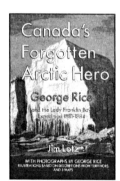
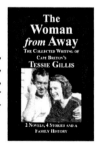